Step Up
and
F.O.C.U.S
(Follow One Course Until Success)
4@13@7
System

By Lindsay Hopkins

Lindsay Hopkins

ISBN-13:978-1480190504

ISBN-10:1480190500

Legal Disclaimers & Notices

This book is presented to you for informational purposes only and is not a substitute for any professional advice. The contents herein are based on the views and opinions of the author and all associated contributors.

While every effort has been made by the author and all associated contributors to present accurate and up to date information within this document, it is apparent that technologies and philosophies rapidly change. Therefore, the author and all associated contributors reserve the right to update the contents and information provided herein as these changes progress. The author and/or all associated contributors take no responsibility for any errors or omissions if such discrepancies exist within this document.

The author and all other contributors accept no responsibility for any consequential actions taken, whether monetary, legal, or otherwise, by any and all readers of the materials provided. It is the reader's sole responsibility to seek professional advice before taking any action on their part.

Readers' results will vary based on their skill level and individual perception of the contents herein, and thus no guarantees, monetarily or otherwise, can be made accurately. Therefore, no guarantees are made.

Lindsay Hopkins

Contents

Lindsay Hopkins

About the Author

I was born in Amersham (Buckinghamshire, England) on the 15th November 1958 into an Army family (mum and dad were both from South Wales). My father had done National Service in the Royal Welch Fusiliers and then taken a commission in the Royal Army Educational Corps; mum had been a WREN and was also a trained opera singer. My first real memory as a child was running wild and free in Nakuru, Kenya whilst dad served with the King's African Rifles, a joyous three-to-four years, a time of space, beautiful countryside, adventures, play and laughter. A brief spell back in Strensall in Yorkshire and then off to even more adventures in Singapore for three years (another great army posting for mum and dad). Three years of heat (which I loved), excitement, smells of the orient, colours and the charm of the Far East.

At the age of 11 I went off to boarding school at the Duke of York's Royal Military School in Dover with about 500 other boys. It was a rugby, cricket, swimming, cross-country running army school, for army orphans and sons of serving soldiers. Some people hate boarding school (like both my sister and my brother), but in truth, barring one short six-week patch at the age of 14, when my father rescued me for an exeat (half day out) and talked me through my "homesick pain," I embraced boarding school life. I loved the sport, the friends and once the regime was understood I knew exactly how to have fun and woke up every day (or most days anyway) with a massive smile on my face. I am lucky I have always had my default mood as that of 100% happiness! I studied hard (we had no choice), swam for the school, played rugby for the school all the way up to the 1st XV and became the Head of School in my last year. A model student, but not a perfect one - I had many a caning and detention on my way through the school I can assure you!

I applied for five universities, Liverpool was my first choice and Oxford and Cambridge were my fourth and fifth choices, which didn't go down well with my tutors. I was given what was known as an unconditional place at Liverpool to study Marine Zoology (I fancied being the second Jacques Cousteau). In my final term at school my headmaster grabbed me into his study and asked me if I fancied "having a bash" at the Regular Commissions Board (RCB) selection at Westbury to become sponsored through the Army at University. I really had no desire to become an Army officer but the idea of being paid whilst I was at University was to me a great one. I passed the RCB first time, much to my amazement.

Liverpool University at the age of 18, after a brief spell at Sandhurst, (Camberley), on what was known as the "one pip wonder course," was total bliss. Great friendships were forged, lots of rugby, lots of parties, lots of relationships and even some lectures. I swapped from Marine Zoology to Psychology after attending a psychology lecture as a guest and I simply fell in love with the subject. I really felt it was far more me. I finally emerged with a very average 2:2 BSc with Honours.

During university I grabbed the chance to go back to my Regiment (the 1st Royal Tank Regiment) whenever I could but also had some great adventures which included "three amigos" busking around Europe on Euro Rail, learning how to be a Mountain Leader in the Highlands of Scotland and learning how to ski for a month in Bavaria with the Army.

Following my graduation I went back to Sandhurst for the full-on course to learn how to be an Army officer. I made more superb friends and almost without exception had a glorious time there for six months. I have no doubt the school experience and military regime helped my mindset. I think the only exception was on the final exercise in South Wales on the Brecon Beacons at 2am in a bleak January when I truly questioned the wisdom of guarding a trench against four sheep whilst the snow fell upon my head. I could not see the benefit of frost bite and hyperthermia while sitting in my own homeland! Luckily the Guards Colour Sergeant who looked after our platoon as an instructor, made me see sense with several slugs of port from his hip flask and some very firm sage words of wisdom. I passed the course and "graduated" again on the main square of Sandhurst, sword in hand, watched by my proud parents and my fiancée to be Chrissy, who I had met whilst on leave over the Christmas period.

I learned the mastery of becoming a Tank Commander at Lulworth and Bovington camp in Dorset for a further six months, together with 30 other armoured corps young officers, but this time the fun was being treated as a semi grown up for the first time. Now we had our commissions and soldiers even had to call us "Sir" and salute us (even if they didn't mean it!). Following Dorset I returned to Germany to where the regiment was based - at that time each regiment in the British Army was about 400/500 men and 60/70 tanks - to a life of fun but relative calm as, luckily for me, there was no real action going on in the world apart from the troubles in Northern Ireland which the regiment did get involved with.

I loved my short time in the army and I made some truly superb friends which have endured through my whole life. But sadly I suffered some form of breakdown and spent two-to-three months in Woolwich Military Hospital where they tried to work out what was wrong with me! I was not well at all and had all the tests you can imagine to fathom why I had "gone off the rails." At one point I was even being challenged for fabricating the "condition" to get out of repaying my university fees and not serving the rest of my Army contract. But four Army Medical Boards soon cleared that concern up, thanks to the support from my father, who was by that time a Colonel. To this day it is not clear what happened. I guess we could call it Post Traumatic Stress Disorder. But to be honest, I have never been inclined to go back and revisit this section of my life. What happened, happened! A tough time I must confess.

The Army Medical Board deemed me unfit for further service in a "teeth arm," (as in front-line soldiering) and so I was given the choice of the Army Pay Corps, the Army Catering Corps or a gratuity and an honourable exit after a set period of continued service. I chose to leave. I did however have nine to 12 months still to serve. I was sent up to work with the great explorer Colonel Blashford Snell, (of Operation Raleigh and Drake fame), up in Fort George, Inverness with the Fort George Volunteers teaching young inner city children how to embrace the highlands.

During this time I had leave to finally marry Chrissy after a cancellation due to illness. We were granted a few days leave in London by the Army, but our main honeymoon was touring the highlands in the guise of conducting a reconnaissance for the following year's Fort George Volunteers in a VW Golf GTI, all expenses paid! It emerged after our two week break that no reconnaissance report was actually required.

I returned for the last time to my regiment at Bovington Camp with Chrissy to commence my gardening leave, where you were allowed as much time off as you needed to hunt for jobs outside the Army. I applied to every FTSE 100 company I could find with an impeccable CV but the mental aberration or medical "blip" prevented any job offers heading my way. My conclusion was that the only way forward was a commission-only role in a financial services company in London. "No training required."I applied and was accepted, (surprise surprise!). So off I went to London town "where the streets are paved with gold."

I must say that I swapped a khaki uniform or rather black tank coveralls really, for the new city uniform - a pin-striped suit, white shirt and silk tie, with ease. I was so excited; we were motivated every day by our enthusiastic managers who were taught to lead by example and so enthusiasm was very high every single day. It was a "lead from the front," "total commitment," "judge by results" environment. The work ethos of "in early, leave late" and a recognition system was enough to stimulate even a dormant polar bear. I loved it - the challenges, the comradeship, the ups and downs and the learning, plus, quite simply, being in "The City." I worked for nine superb years in the Porchester Group, which then morphed into the MI Group and finally City Financial. I rose from Trainee Consultant to Branch Manager in 18 months and then started to build a team of sales people who worked under me for override commission. The team size increased from one to about 40 in a two-year period. I think I ended up as a Senior Branch Manager and so from recruit, (I was recruit number 97), the company grew to 3,000- plus strong nationwide.

Luckily I stayed ahead of the pack and was one of the top 10 managers. I won loads of conventions, as all the good people did, which entailed five-star trips with your partner once a year all around the world: San Francisco, Los Angeles, Hawaii, the Caribbean, Singapore, Bali, Australia and many more far flung destinations. But sadly when the original CEO and gladiator left us under a cloud my heart left the business too. A hard wrench for me as loyalty was one of our USPs, but the love of the role left me.

I was headhunted into the infamous Allied Dunbar with lots of promises and a large cheque, as long as I brought my team with me, which I did; in the main in a "top secret" operation over one Easter Holiday. I was blanked by all my friends who I left behind but I was sure it was the right move for me. I adored the six courses of one-to-two week management training we had to do down in the residential training centre in Swindon and I loved the learning. We were taught all the aspects of business management, coaching styles, interview techniques and selection methods. I quite simply lapped all this information up and applied it within my daily running of the branch in Haymarket (near Trafalgar Square).

I was becoming fed up with managing and coaching sales people who were earning more than me. It seemed like far more fun to actually run a practice and get out there selling to clients and be able to build a practice that actually had a value to sell after a few years. So with permission from my senior director I emerged over the course of a year from being a manager to setting up my own practice, Trafalgar Square Financial Planning Consultants (within Allied Dunbar), with a small team. I did well and enjoyed more conventions, awards and accolades.

At the time though there was only one place to work if you were fully qualified and a reasonable salesperson/adviser, which I had become, and that was The Rothschild Partnership and they had been chatting with me for some years. I moved with a nice joining fee, (a bit like a footballer), and enjoyed a further two years in what then became known as the St James'

Place Partnership. I must mention this was not without a High Court case raised against me by Allied Dunbar which was beaten off soundly! At Rothschild we were dealing with wealth management and high net worth individuals with a tremendous focus on customer care, service and spending time with clients, which I loved. It was less about the numbers through the door, and more about building up long-term relationships. It was great fun, great learning and very, very civilized, and just around the corner from the Bank of England in the heart of the City.

In the autumn of 2002 one or two things were bugging me and despite the scare tactics of the big companies telling us that it's cold out there if we go out on our own, I simply needed to find out if this was true. My sales figures were dropping but my own mortgage business, which I was allowed to run in conjunction with being a partner in St James,' was going OK, I parted company in a civilized and amicable way unlike my two previous very frosty experiences.

So there I was on the 23rd December 2002 with a new business to start and a garden shed! So that's where Trafalgar Square Financial Planning Consultants really started. Whilst initially I could only advise on mortgages, I moved into the full Independent Financial Adviser role some time later. I had one aim and that was to be my own boss and earn a healthy six figures to support my family. That worked in year one and with the help of two tremendously loyal people in my team, and some very good support from friends and family, things took shape beautifully.

From 2003 to 2007 turnover doubled every year and the company size grew from three to nigh on 27. I worked tirelessly but had great fun and during 2003-2006 built a business to business company called Trafalgar Square Solutions which packaged mortgages for other brokers, an Overseas Mortgage Company called Trafalgar Square Overseas and offshore investment company: Trafalgar Square Investments which focused on offshore property funds. Life was good, busy, and profitable and of course, varied.

There was synergy between all the companies and so the multi-company concept was not terrifying, and I had a very solid team to support everything, and the infrastructure was there. I was very lucky to work with some great people. Around 2006 I also set up a bridging finance company with a business partner, (the first ever Secret Millionaire, Gill Fielding), called Secure the Bridge.

Way back in 2003/2004 I had been invited by an old client of mine from the Rothschild days to be a guest speaker and trainer with a property education company and so I became a regular speaker with Whitney UK, (today known as Tigrent). The training appearances increased over the years to the point where for at least five-to-six weekends a year I was on my feet co–presenting a course known as Creative Finance for upwards of 50–60 individuals at a time.

This exposure and experience initiated requests from individuals for a little more than financial advice, more on coaching concepts which suited me down to the ground as this was at the heart of what I really wanted to do. The Creative Finance course became more and more personal development focussed from my point of view and so the coaching side of things simply evolved naturally. The financial services world always demanded a very pro-positive mindset and so from that point on in my life I engaged a coach once a month to help me move forward.

Weaved in amongst all this I had been asked to become a parent Governor at Swaffield Primary school where my son had been at school and after three years became appointed as Chair of Governors, a position I held for just over ten years. I also joined the Association of International Property Professionals due to my link with overseas mortgages. I joined the board and subsequently became elected chairman of this board for two enjoyable years. Not easy running a board of 18 feisty overseas property entrepreneurs I can tell you, but it yielded invaluable business experience and great contacts.

I think many books have been written about what happened to the economy between 2008 and 2010 but needless to say it was carnage and the financial services aspects of my businesses, particularly mortgages, saw bloodshed and mayhem with a 70% downturn in turnover literally overnight! No-one was left unscathed and whilst I had seen recessions I had never been a business owner during one of these events before. We had many casualties and no one escaped unscarred. We held on to the lifeboats and kept rowing! I lost some businesses, and sadly lost some friendships, but everyone was fighting for their lives. I certainly don't hold any grudges and I hope none are harboured against me. I have always had good friends around me, and good support from my family, and so we resolved not to throw the towel in. But thank goodness I had decided to diversify.

Today

I am living with my wife and son in London. My daughter has finally "flown the coop." I pursue my businesses with passion and I love the mixture of coaching, speaking, property and finance which keeps me continually stimulated. I embrace life I have great fun and pursue my goals with energy and focus 99.99% of the time.

My Current Business Activities

Trafalgar Square Financial Planning Consultants (TSFPC) (www.trafalgarsq.co.uk) holds strong and whilst somewhat shrunken in size since 2007, it still retains the position as one of the niche suppliers of buy-to-let mortgages in the UK. It remains in a healthy position.

Trafalgar Square Overseas Ltd (www.trafalgarsqoverseas.co.uk) - is an overseas mortgage business which is alive and kicking and now specialises more in building and launching small niche, alternative and unregulated collective investments.

Secure the Bridge (www.securethebridge.com) - is a short term bridging finance company which services in the main the clients of TSFPC, focusing on the buy-to-let market and this has been going from strength to strength over the last few years.

C & M Wealth (www.cmwealthgroup.com) –is a group of international committed professionals whose main focal point is to provide a specially made consultancy service for high net worth individuals around the world who want to invest in the UK. It also provides personal development, business coaching and a one stop shop settling and relocation service.

Coaching and Training:

Future Performance Coaching (**www.futureperfomancecoaching.com**) -is a private coaching business for my own clients which has been operating since 2007 and grows from strength to strength.

The T60 Coaching Program (**www.t60coaching.com**) - is currently a specialist high-intensity coaching programme offered exclusively to Tigrent clients, provided by a team of specialist coaches which I co-ordinate, with a partner, focusing on property and business.

Millionaire Action Plans (M.A.P.s) -is a membership mastermind business and property support group involving aspiring entrepreneurs who want to get going quickly with the right sort of grass roots support.

I run private seminars/workshops through the year and still present as a speaker with many of the courses with Tigrent each year. I am on the UK Property Network circuit as a keynote speaker and I like to be 'on my feet' for one of these events at least once a month.

Life is busy, fruitful and rewarding and it allows me to have multiple income streams, a platform for creativity and the continuity to "Step Up and F.O.C.U.S." (Follow One Course Until Successful) ensuring I apply "4@13@7" to my everyday life.

Testimonials

"Lindsay personalised the coaching to my needs. Lindsay made everything more organised, more specific and more defined. Lindsay is a special individual who has the ability to help a stone jump off a cliff if it felt it was necessary in moving forward. Lindsay is a teacher, helper, coach, inspirational, motivator."

Vincent Pretorius

"Since working with Lindsay my confidence levels have increased dramatically. He was honest, taking in all aspects of my life to ensure I could then focus on the goals which were most important to me. It is well documented that those who seek ongoing coaching are more likely to succeed than those who go it alone and Lindsay is truly there to help achieve your dreams. Success follows success. Lindsay walks the talk. He coaches from personal success not text book learning. He is fun, honest and successful."

Diane Goulding.

"Lindsay is an amazing coach especially in helping one to succeed quickly in reaching one's goals. He cares deeply and is committed to one's success. Lindsay is a very positive person who encourages you to be solution-orientated and look at issues in a different way. He gives you confidence with positive attitude and shows you that you can make it happen – no matter how busy you are! He is soulful, authentic and dynamic."

Marie Sheehan

"One of the first things Lindsay helps you to do is to find out where you are in the different parts of your life. After you discover yourself, you can start formalising your goals. Lindsay helped me to change my dreams into goals. He made me think about them and write them down! He uses many ways to stay focused: pictures, affirmations, stepping stones, self assessment. I really like that Lindsay makes you accountable to what you said you want to achieve in a certain time and just love that he stresses the power of celebration when you achieve something."

Monika Kubis

Foreword

By Gill Fielding, 'Secret Millionaire'

When Lindsay asked me to write this foreword I immediately felt motivated as I knew then that I was going to get an advance copy and be able to read what he has been writing recently. I was motivated because I had that same honour before, so I knew what I was about to receive, read and digest would be something fabulous and of real interest to me.

As I read it I instantly 'felt' the grit in the book – the sense of purpose and it reminded me that Lindsay is a character full of determination, perseverance and consistency and that character comes across in the guidance and information he provides.

Life is full of ups and downs and what this book creates is a sense of structure to deal logically with whatever life throws as us. It's a discipline and a process and we can see and feel a sense of striving for the pocket of excellence within all of us. It's remarkable that such a powerful sense of purpose is capable of being produced by mere words.

As usual Lindsay keeps on growing and developing and he has a real sense of personal perfection, and he clearly wants that for himself and for others – this is a selfless book and I often feel that for Lindsay it's better to facilitate greatness for others than it is for himself.

He gives very freely of his time and expertise and he knows the personal development world to its very core – without one single doubt there will be something in this book that helps you whatever your particular challenge may be.

It's rare to find a book that reveals so much about its author and Lindsay's personality and character shines throughout as you read. There's a sense of drive and organisation and almost military precision and time keeping (no surprise there then!!) It's a great book, a great read and a great set of tools.

By Steve Smith

When I wrote a foreword for Lindsay's first book I shared how we met, how our friendship has grown over the years and my opinions of the man. Since meeting Lindsay in 1977 at Liverpool University and me making my initial opinion, which has stuck, of a creative, good fun, loyal and full of lust for life which left most individuals standing and of course becoming a good friend of mine, sharing misdemeanors and adventures, we have embarked on further adventures together and he has excelled as I anticipated above and beyond. He remains driven, motivated and sincere in the workplace and still strikes me as motivated, a loyal friend, caring towards other people, loving to his family and still a man with inspiring passion for life, laughter and fun.

His many years in business have not changed him dramatically despite the bumps and stumbles he has had along the way, which at times allowed unhappiness to seep into his life he remained throughout a professional sales manager, a motivator of people, a caring leader, a creative manager and a great value-based sales person. After leaving behind the world of the city to set up in his garden shed and then build a team of 27+ and use the lessons he had learned and sticking to his values, I mentioned he struck me as passionate, committed to success and a man with vision, I stand by this.

He has continued to build upon his business, surviving the shrinking of his team during issues of 2005 to 2011, which hit him, hard. We went into business together with an offshore property fund for a while, he started speaking at property training courses, progressing with his coaching and mentoring programmes, all of which I think really helped him weather the storms. Around this time was when I sensed a change in him. His true passions and path were emerging, he loved helping people and was now enjoying the coaching and mentoring more than anything. Despite being battered by the credit crunch he remained resilient, creative and completely unwilling to accept that he should compromise on his goals, I continue to respect this.

Since writing his first book he continues with his path in life, he has started investing in property in Wales with a business partner and his new business C&M wealth which incorporates his experience in personal development, coaching and corporate business is flourishing nicely.

Now one piece of advice I once gave in an interview was to read everything. I believe that to be informed helps your choices and your decision processes. Lindsay lives in a world of coaching, positive motivation and guiding people. I am involved in a different world but I respect his total commitment to share and help people move forward.

I respect what Lindsay has done in this book. His first book started people on the journey to think about that they wanted and actually craft goals this takes things so much deeper it's actually fascinating to read. What is great is that these are not just theories and ideas which he has plucked from thin air. These are his tried and tested methods which he has used and he has shared with his coaching clients to great success over the last few years. So in effect it is a tried and tested template for success in any endeavour. The most important element to his 4@13@7 system is it creates certainty of focus, it ensures people stay on track but even more than that it builds in a chance to fail a little bit along the way, make mistakes but still succeed in the end. This gives a reality to setting goals and achieving them. This can become a way of life for a lot of people who are bent on success and who have been floundering for the right method.

Lindsay and I are lifelong friends and when I was asked to write the forward for his first book I was very honoured. To be asked a second time is an even bigger honour.

How to use this book

It is not for me to tell you how to read this book, but I ask your permission to give you some pointers. Each chapter is made up of sections which have some exercises you can complete for yourself, please do have a go, it will help the words and ideas come alive for you and take on true meaning. At the end of each chapter you will see a mind map which summaries what has been covered and it may help you to come to your own conclusions about whether to adopt or discard the information you have read. You will find that each chapter has a story about one of my coaching clients which has relevance to the particular chapter you have just read. You will also see a list of five affirmations which you may wish to use and adopt to help re-enforce the affirmation of the strategies and ideas I have shared with you.

Enjoy the book, it is written to help you achieve greater success in your goal planning, but more to the point in your goal successes.

<u>Why I wrote this book</u>

They do say there is a book in everyone and so in theory when I wrote and published my first book *'Step up and FOCUS'* perhaps that could have been it! However, when I started to go out and about presenting the contents of my first book it became obvious that I had simply exposed another layer of managing goals to ensure the best possible chance of them being achieved.

The first step is of course to understand yourself; to gain full self-awareness on how you communicate, learn and what your strength and weaknesses are. This leads naturally to identifying your true core values, thus establishing your goals with a regular review process. This first step is a giant step and one that some people never take. However, beyond this is the need to manage and monitor and adjust these goals as you go through your journey.

I identified whilst working with thousands of people who I train, teach and coach that we have to go all the way. By that I mean we need to plan exactly what our expectations are all the way through the year. That is precisely what this book does. "4 @13@7" is a methodology which I have used successfully and shared with a large number of my coaching clients. It is a protocol; it is a simple system to align the goals and more to the point the actions. First, to identify the needs, then to accomplish the goals and finally to monitor them before framing them accurately. Some might say the "4@13@7" system is a little too detailed.

> **ANNUAL GOALS > 4 QUARTERS > 13 WEEKS > 7 DAYS**

I fundamentally disagree. It allows you to integrate your goals and goal actions into your everyday life.

Have fun. Enjoy reading this book as much as I enjoyed writing it. But most importantly try it out. Try out the methodology. You will be impressed with your own results.

<u>Acknowledgments</u>

I am still yet to win that BAFTA or BRIT Award and it is still not really a goal of mine. However, I do want to say a few thank yous like that of an acceptance speech, as without the people who have so far been involved in my 54-year journey I would not quite be the man that I am.

I have spent time pondering once more on whom to mention and thank and I know there are people I have missed out. It is not through malice and if you are part of my journey you have made a contribution and I do thank you for that.

I would like to thank:

➢ My wife Chrissy for her endless patience with my passion for hard work and using up every 24 hour period with action!

➢ My lovely daughter Gabby who fills my life with light and who helped me put this book together.

➢ My beautiful son Daniel who never fails to surprise me in his adventures.

➢ My dog Ollie who gives me unconditional love and helps my creativity as we walk the parks and streets of the Borough of Wandsworth.

- My fantastic mother Molly Hopkins who has and always will be full of care, love and support for her children.

- My great father Ron Hopkins who has been a father and friend all my life.

- My sister Belinda who remains a constant inspiration to me.

- My brother Jon who always has and always will make me laugh with a wit and repartee second to none.

- My daughter's Godfather Timothy John Orchard who has been a rock for me for most of my adult life.

- My Trafalgar Square partner Sarah Jane Costello and her husband Richard (deceased) who helped me onto the springboard of building my own businesses back in 2003.

- My personal assistant Jeannie Woollen for her undying loyalty, her sense of humour and patience.

- To my coach Pam Richards who helps me beyond belief all the time.

- ➢ To everyone who works in any business that I am involved in. I am lucky to work with you.

- ➢ To Mark (Sweets) Dalton who co-presents with me and has coached with me for ten years of solid friendship, fun and laughs.

- ➢ To Sean Thomson, my property business partner, who is focused, fair and fun.

- ➢ To all the T60 coaches whom I love working with and continue to learn from.

- ➢ To all the partners in M.A.Ps who continue to keep me on my metal.

- ➢ To all my past and present coaching clients who help me to realise that giving is better than receiving.

- ➢ To my partner in Secure The Bridge: Gill Fielding, for continued help, support and grounding.

- ➢ To the CEO of Tigrent Learning UK: Iain Edwards who changed my world with one simple conversation over a beer.

➢ To Ming and Chang in C & M Wealth who kept nagging me to build a business with them.

➢ To my dear friend Jim Hawkins (deceased) who lives on my right shoulder as a guardian and reminds me all the time that it is the journey that counts not the destination.

➢ My oldest and dearest pal, Steven Miles Smith who generates laughter at every turn.

➢ To Carluccio's chain of restaurants (Putney) where I have sat and written a great deal of this book sitting by the River Thames.

Chapter One

<u>The Rucksack!!!</u>

"You cannot change something that has happened to you. But you can change the way you feel about it."

The quote above is I am sure not original and I would not claim it as mine albeit it is my mixture of words. For me the way we carry our past with us, based on our experiences both positive and negative, is key to how we move forward. It is quite simple, the negatives can place the breaks on the pace of progress and the positives can help to fuel or turbo-charge our way forward.

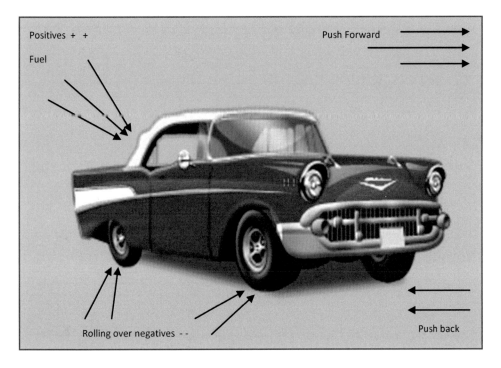

We therefore need to be extremely mindful of these factors if we are going to become *Masters of Our Own Future* or *Warriors of Our Own Life*.

There is of course a catch. Going forwards we can learn to control and filter the way we feel about the events that happen in our life, before they get filed away into our sub-conscious mind. As you well know, this filing away happens as we sleep.

I think it's described in computer terms as "clean up" or "defragging." As we slumber, all the events of the day are analysed, sifted and stored. But my point is that with knowledge and a positive process we can ensure that this filing.

FROM NOW ON!

Can be filed correctively and positively framed.

BUT!

What about the "things" that have happened before?

In my case at the tender age of 54 let us assume I have misfiled events that have happened to me all my "mature life," let's say from the ages of 20-53.

This is: 33x365=12,045

So this could possibly be 12,045 misfiled days of my life, fuelling my sub-conscious going forward! This is a potentially scary thought. Look, I am not saying that everything is filed away negatively, but I tend to refer to this Jamboree bag of experiences, negatively stored as someone's *"Rucksack."* If you ponder upon this, our rucksack must be one of our frames of reference for all conscious decisions we make. It is our wisdom resource.

KNOWLEDGE + EXPERIENCE = WISDOM

It is then, with this wisdom, we make decisions. So reflecting back to the equation:

$$K + E = W$$

One needs to consider how we file the experience and how we frame it, how we place it into our knowledge bank. So let's just consider a few examples of some outcomes which you cannot change but with a variety of possibilities, you can change how you feel about them.

Business experience......

.........I was pitching to a training company for the license to run a specifically tailored coaching programme some years ago. I was in fact going head-to-head against someone who was far more powerful and experienced than me in the "universe." This pitch I was involved in, the competition also knew me and was aware of the dual pitch and that only one could be the winner. During this process, prior to the pitch going forward I received a phone call. I don't think it is appropriate to quote the call word for word but essentially I was asked in no uncertain terms to "back off or else." The "or else" was potentially not only the loss of new business but the loss of several other accounts!!!

So what way to turn, left or right? Restrain what I have and at least stay safe? Respond to a threat from someone I knew was more than capable of making my life difficult!!!

What did my rucksack tell me – based on......$K + E = W$

Well the situation required some swift decision making. So I posed myself some questions.

If I ignore this threat:

Does it slow me down towards achieving my goals? Yes/No?	YES
Is it in synergy with what I want to achieve? Yes/No?	YES
Does it stifle me? Yes/No?	NO
Does it serve me? Yes/No?	YES

If I accept the threat and back off!!! If I asked myself the same question, then what (see above)?

By the way I had a certain element of fear here. I am not a fearless warrior. Yet, there was clarity of purpose taking me forward which I could not ignore. That was my series of goals. What did my rucksack tell me?

So what happened? I ignored the threat, carried on with the pitch and won the license and have been running the coaching programme involved for four years now, with a business partner and a selection of other coaches, very successfully. I think there are minor crunch points in our life and there are major crunch points in our life. Our rucksack is bound to affect all our decisions but it is of course all the more important when it's a biggie. The questions I posed to myself helped me:

> ➤ **Does this slow me down towards achieving my goals?**
> ➤ **Is it in synergy with what I want to achieve and on course with my values?**
> ➤ **Does it stifle me?**
> ➤ **Does it serve me?**

You might wish to use these four questions to help you when you are making decisions.

By the way, my frame of reference from my rucksack once I had posed these questions to myself, my strength and my confidence to proceed came from my "mouldy orange" experience, way back when I was 15 or 16 years old. I was in the fifth form at an army boarding school. It was the first term of the year; the new sixth formers were learning to flex their muscles (metaphorically speaking) with authority and their new found positions as prefects. The school was divided up into eight houses of around 50 boys in each. The senior houses had an age range of 13 to 18. The school was highly disciplined but mostly fair. One of our many tasks was what was known as a "litter sweep." All the junior years, around 13 to 16 from each house would walk around the allocated area around our accommodation building and pick up litter, making the school "spick and span." Each litter sweep was controlled by two or three prefects. I generally did not mind this chore, respected the rules and I was as proud of our house, Roberts House, as the next person.

Sourced from http://weheartit.com

So there we were, 20 to 30 of us spread out picking up litter and rubbish, wandering around in a gaggle, when I heard a shout, "Oi, Hopkins, you have missed something." This sixth form prefect, let's call him MS, was a newly appointed prefect, only one year older than me and renowned for being a bully! I was shown that I had missed picking up a disgusting mouldy orange which was in a flower bed. I was quite popular and so some interest was aroused amongst the rest of the third, fourth and fifth years, as we generally didn't pick up stuff that was 'organically absorbable' like a mouldy orange! I politely pointed this out to MS. He was insistent, and of course with a crowd gathering this was becoming a major issue for him and for me. If I backed down I would be humiliated and vice versa. I genuinely felt this was unreasonable! A minor 'fracas' in the big scheme of things, but compliance to a renowned bully would set a precedent for the rest of the school year. MS called for some support from other sixth formers and with the crowd of third, fourth and fifth formers and now a few sixth formers watching, I was physically forced down upon the mouldy orange. My nose ceremoniously being rubbed in it I was asked five times to pick it up. I declined tears of humiliation rolling down my cheeks but I would not succumb to this blonde, six foot bully. Insolence towards sixth formers was a major offence and of course I was being cursed and threatened during this, what must have been only a ten minutes battle of will power. I do need to share that:

"I did not pick up the orange!!!"

Petty, pathetic and so minor indeed however, the story resonated around the school and despite my tears and apparent humiliation it was seen that there was only one loser....MS! I was not punished further and I learned that you can face down a bully.

A silly story? Well, yes and no! I still recall the mouldy orange moment as one of my *"The Rucksack"* moments to remind myself that despite the fear threats and bullies seldom expect to be challenged, it was that knowledge that helped me countless times in my life including during my coaching pitch.

I had the honour and privilege of addressing a conference of four hundred plus people in 2011. I was co presenting with one of my partners who is in the acknowledgments at the front of this book. I was keen to illustrate *"The Rucksack"* concept so I walked on stage with a rucksack and a whole set of baked bean cans covered in white paper clearly labelled with some supposedly "bad" things that had happened in my life. I took them out and shared them with the audience.

These are but a few:-

Boss ran off with £120,000.

Best friend committed suicide.

15 County Court Judgments.

High Court summons for "theft."

Hospitalised and medically discharged from the army as a career officer.

I actually pulled out 18 baked bean cans! I asked one or two of the audience to try and lift the loaded rucksack and to walk up and down the aisle of the conference. They found it difficult and I am not surprised! My point is that it is not easy to carry this weight with you; furthermore it is bound to slow you down!!

So what should we do? How can we make sure we do not carry this rucksack with us? I actually think we need to not allow anything to **enter** *"The Rucksack."* In fact why don't we resolve not to have one?! Before we make this decision let's look at two of the baked bean cans I mentioned to look at how they can be dealt with.

When we are confronted with some potential rucksack contents to carry around and try to weigh us down we really need to do this process. It is a case of asking a few questions of ourselves.

- ➢ How do I really feel about this?
- ➢ What can I learn from this?
- ➢ How can I best frame this to serve me in the future?

So be brave! Write down ten things that have happened to you in your life which may be sitting in your rucksack.

Go through the three questions:-

> ➢ How do I really feel about this?
> ➢ What can I learn from this?
> ➢ How can I best frame this to serve me in the future?

I am not asking you to dwell on history or unpick past issues to create pain. However, if you want to move forward you have to "let go" and stay light and nimble mentally. In the future do not even have *"The Rucksack"* just take experiences and positively frame them, then move on with greater wisdom.

"The Rucksack Story"

Sarah had a superb CV, a 1st at Oxford University and offers of positions at the top five legal firms in the UK. She had a great job earning a healthy £60-80K per annum in a specialist freelance contract she had landed. When Sarah took one of the tests I use with my coaching clients called the confidence calculator she scored 8/80, the lowest score I had ever seen.

When I sit down with my coaching clients we always set a series of objectives to ensure that we can track results. Sarah only had one objective which was to become confident, we agreed that a jump from 8/80 to 40/80 would be a good start.

It appeared that *"The Rucksack"* she was carrying around was an upbringing by parents for whom nothing was "good enough," this was perpetuating by her now long term boyfriend.

Sarah set about removing *"The Rucksack;"* she did in fact extract herself from her long term relationship, she controlled her communication with her mother and she set about some hard talks to push confidence boundaries. She was excited, determined and persistent in her objective and she worked hard.

This was no mean feat, the creation of mental freedom, the acceptance that one has to fail to succeed (a tough one), and to overcome the fear of a barrage of judgemental comments.

This hard work involved crafting her life deliberately, making a physical effort to surround herself with loving people.

It involved a pursuit of new and stimulating hobbies and interests, as well as a whole series of self monitoring and accountability protocols and systems so she stayed on track.

Six months down the line, Sarah bravely re-took the confidence test; funnily enough on her prompting, not mine. She scored 65/80: a massive jump, through her hard work and stickabilty. She had changed her physical appearance, she smiled more, walked taller and she was in her own words significantly happier.

Sometimes *"The Rucksack"* is very heavy and more to the point people help you, possibly even insist on you carrying it with you. Sometimes they will even remind you not to forget your *"Rucksack!!!!"* What I saw here was someone who was determined to look forward, prepared to take action to change and leave *"The Rucksack"* behind!!!

Summary

➢ Knowledge and Experience = Wisdom (K + E = W)

➢ Ask yourself <u>four</u> questions to do with decisions and the situation.

➢ Consider your existing *"Rucksack,"* is it full?

➢ Empty your *"Rucksack,"* re-frame it to make it lighter or get rid of it all together.

➢ Look at negative and positive framing.

➢ Do not have a *"Rucksack"* going forward.

Rucksack Affirmations

➢ *I am always looking forward to what I can achieve.*

➢ *I am always focusing on the future.*

➢ *I am always asking myself the positive questions to ensure my decisions serve me.*

➢ *I am working to understand how knowledge and experiences can give me wisdom.*

➢ *I am constantly aware that I should only work on what I can change.*

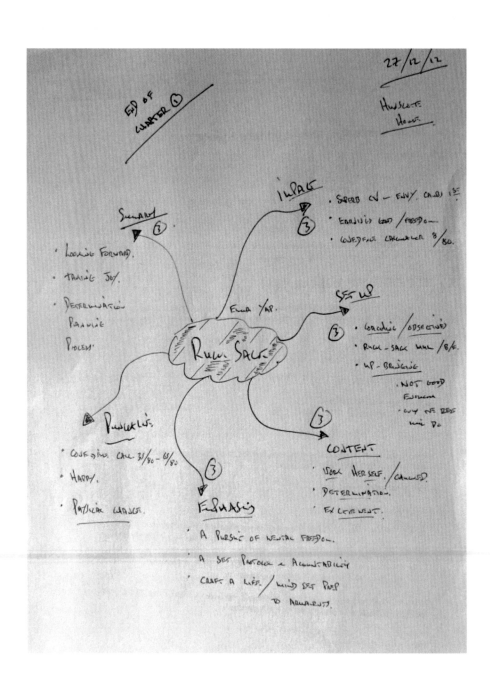

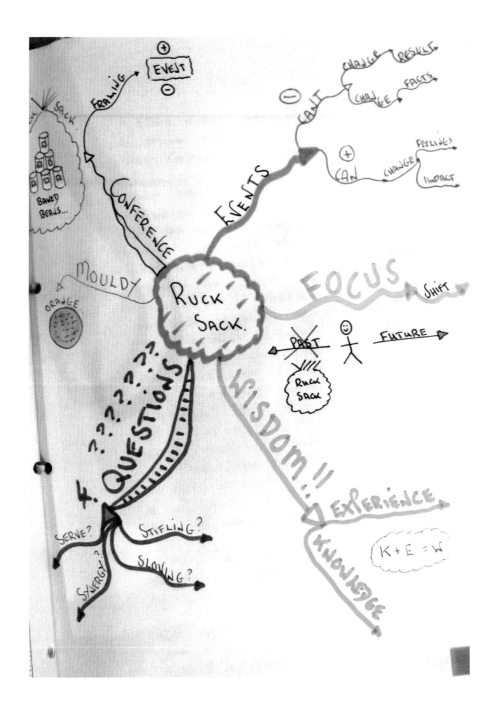

Chapter 2

<u>GOALS</u>

"A person without goals is like a sailing ship setting out from port without a destination."

I have read more books and attended more seminars on establishing goals and achieving goals than anything else in my life. I truly believe in the quote above. I see someone without clear goals, as a person just drifting (or sailing) with little purpose, or indeed becoming part of someone else's purpose or goal. This of course, for a lot of people with jobs, that is exactly what happens.

There are a great many ways to illicit goals from your mind on to paper (yes you must always write them down) and to be honest I don't think that one method stands out over the rest, so the "goal gurus" are right. So my very point is that as long as you do it, as long as you follow a process to map out what you want, that is great.

There is however, one step before establishing your goals and that is to ensure that you understand your values and indeed understand your value hierarchy as in, which are the most important and which are the least important. I covered this area in depth in my first book *"Step up and FOCUS."* Let me bring it in the flow of the story in this book. You will see a list of potential values plus some gaps for you to enter you own words.

The game is you can only choose 10!!!

GFH©

Belief	Humility	Respect
Balance	Imagination	Responsibility
Determination	Independence	Safety
Directness	Influence	Self-awareness
Discipline	Integrity	Self-reliance
Education	Intuition	Self-respect
Effort	Joy	Sensitivity
Elegance	Justice	Spirituality
Empowerment	Kindness	Stability
Enthusiasm	Love	Success
Equality	Loyalty	Tact
Excellence	Morality	Tenacity
Fairness	Modesty	Tolerance
Focus	Moderation	Tradition
Freedom	Optimism	Trust
Friendliness	Organisation	Understanding
Fun	Patience	Vision
Financial security	Peace	Wonder
Family	Pride	Wealth
Growth	Prudence	Wisdom
Generosity	Perfection	1.
Happiness	Pleasure	2.
Harmony	Power	3.
Health	Quality	4.
Honesty	Recognition	5.

Now list the top 10 values below. Now no matter how hard it is, place them priority. Ranking 1 to 10, well done!! You now have your values hierarchy!!

1.		6.	
2.		7.	
3.		8.	
4.		9.	
5.		10.	

You can see what is interesting is that if your goals are in synergy or alignment with you. You give yourself a far better chance in achieving them. Also this reduces stress. One of the principal causes of stress is when you are working, living or taking action in conflict with your values.

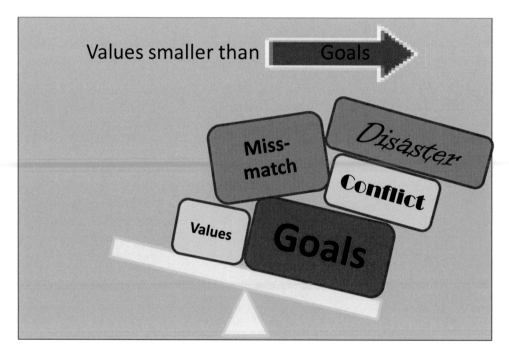

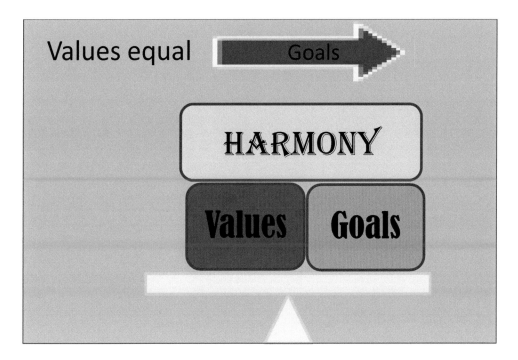

OK, so now we have our values, we know the least important and most important, so now let's look at goal setting briefly. This is not another goal setting book. The purpose of the book is to give you practical tools to maximise your ability and to cultivate the goals once they are set; but let me just share with you how you might do the goal setting. We want to take stock of where we are now. Where we want to "**be**" in the future, may "**be.**" I tend to look at goals as what do you wish to "**be, have** and **do,**" I tend to look at goal areas, a number of areas in your life. So let us take stock! Why not grade where you are on a scale of 1 to 10, in the areas 1 being not so good and 10 being excellent.

Let's map it out.

	1	2	3	4	5	6	7	8	9	10
Health & fitness										
Finances (financial control)										
Family (direct & indirect)										
Education or personal development										
Charitable or community giving										
Spiritual & well being										
Social life & leisure										
Career & business										

OK so we have a potential gap analysis established where you are now. I am guessing scoring 10/10 in each would be ideal. However, let's try to increase your score by one in each. For each, look at how they feel, sound and look like to you. Have a go at describing in two sentences or a few words, "sound bites" what this looks, feels, and sounds, like to you?

Let me give you an example! I have just looked at the next 12 months.

1. **I will lose a stone of weight over the next 12 months by swimming four times a week!**

2. I will always pay myself first and I will save 10% of all I earn.
3. I will have one get together (adventure!) with my family every month.
4. I will read or listen to one personal development book a month over the next 12 months.
5. I will give 50% of all my CD sales to my chosen charity *Make a Wish* this year.
6. I will take time out after every seminar or workshop to give myself "me time" or "down time."
7. I will make active efforts to see, spend time and communicate with my 12 favourite friends.
8. I will create and design one new income stream in the next 12 months.

Now you have a go!

1.

2.

3.

4.

5.

6.

7.

8.

Here is an example:

	1	2	3	4	5	6	7	8	9	10
Health & fitness						☺				
Finances (financial control)			☺							
Family (direct & indirect)						☺				
Education or personal development							☺			
Charitable or community giving						☺				
Spiritual & well being						☺				
Social life & leisure						☺				
Career & business							☺			
Score :				4		30	14			

Total: 48/80

So the score is 48/80. I am aware the instinct is to want to leap to 80/80 but what you can do is set about nudging your way forward in each area with let's say an annual goal. In the example above, a change from 48/80 to 56/80 a jump of one per area of my life would be quite a significant achievement, do you not think? So if your life goal gap 48/80 to 80/80 but you want to feel good, to ensure we are <u>not</u> trying to bite off more than we can chew we are going to go from 48/80 to 54/80.

Let's put this into context. Goals are bound to be as follows:

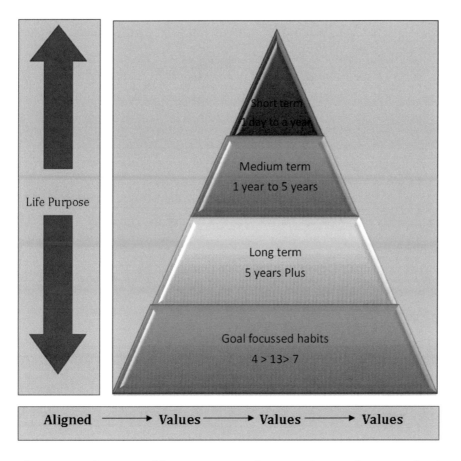

Short, medium and long term; what we have done so far is take a life balance audit, indentified a gap and in the example I gave you the gap is between 48/80 and 80/80.

In the example, I have prompted you to look at shifting from 48/80 to 56/80, this shift is a logical step, to look at and to set up goals over let's say, 12 months short term. You can and should of course consider goals in the short, medium and long term areas. Some people do this with a vision board, some with mind maps and some with some form of goal journal or diary.

My vision board.

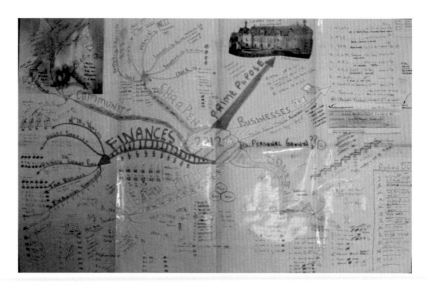

My mind map for 2012.

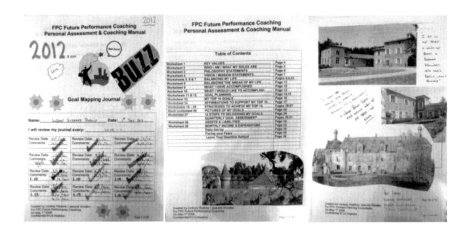

My goal Journal for 2012.

You are simply asking yourself across all the areas in life what do you want to be, do and have in your life?

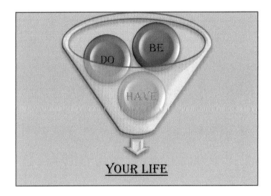

I must stress something here, confidence and momentum comes from achieving goals and moving forward. The key is:

 **_Baby Steps NOT Giant Steps_**  ©GFH

I cannot emphasise this enough! If you try taking giant steps and fail sometimes you will actually reduce your confidence and be stopped in your tracks. You will feel silly, you will feel a failure, you will mentally punish yourself and this could even stop you setting goals again! I have been there and done that. So getting this right is <u>vital</u> in order to ensure that you achieve goals and in essence that is what "4@13@7" is all about. Structure your goals so that they can be achieved and structured. Then to ensure that you have a self-accountability process which will help you monitor progress and allow you to see, feel, hear your successes as you **move forward!**

WOW! This is serious! Of course it is! It is <u>you</u> taking control of your life!

Goals Story

Sebastian started working with me some years ago and his story was a superb one. He had had experiences as an officer in the Rifles, climbed the ladder in the corporate world in the city with producing a great income and created a solid capital base. From the outside looking in, he was in an enviable position, indeed.

The reason Sebastian came to me for coaching was to gain some specific guidance and reassurance on some property projects, where I had some experience. He also wanted some structures and projects to use to build his new life now that he had stepped away from the "city life."

We worked hard on the project analysis itself and the identification of the steps needed. This in itself was simply Sebastian applying existing skills to a new arena. Underneath all of this, as with all my clients, we were working on values, goals, life balance and ensuring that we (he) understood why he was doing all of this. It was a discovery that he wanted to be far more than simply a "bread winner," working every hour God sends and occasionally seeing his wife and family in a state of total exhaustion.

What emerged was something quite extraordinary and exciting for Sebastian. By taking an x-ray of his life, his values and taking time he suddenly had some major revelations. He had never really taken the step to include his family and his children into his goals, he had simply had business and income goals and that was It.

The discovery that his life balance had been so stifled brought not only tears but a tremendous excitement about the freedom he could now achieve in the future. He adopted a completely new perspective of what he wanted to be, have and do. He embraced his family in the most refreshing way I have ever seen.

So this enviable man from the "Gathering of Chattels" perspective discovered deep riches beneath his feet. By goal setting across the whole of his life, he discovered that by taking a wide angle lens to look at this life he could take control and achieve what he wanted without detriment to everything else. A happy man had been born.

Summary

- Goals <u>must</u> be in synergy with your values.

- Consider your hierarchy of values.

- Establish where you are <u>now</u> and where you want to be.

- Plan the baby steps whilst being aware of short, medium and long term goals.

- Vision boards – mind maps – journals.

- Protect your confidence.

Goals Affirmations

- *I am regularly linking my core values to my goals.*

- *I am always reviewing my goals.*

- *I am using mind maps and vision boards to aid me in keeping my goals "alive."*

- *I am always prepared to adjust and review my goals.*

- *I am a goal focused person.*

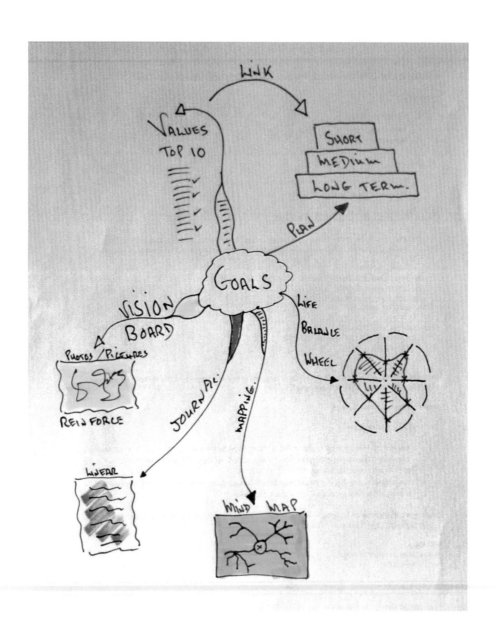

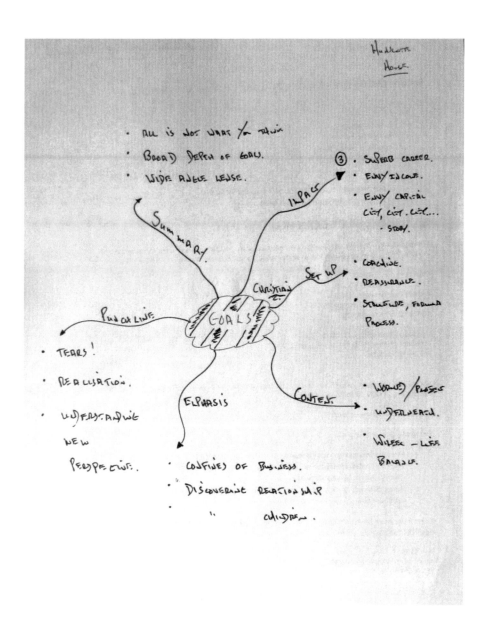

Chapter 3
<u>Relapse</u>

"It defies human nature, but we must build our failure into our success plan!"

It is now time to look at the 4 @13@7 concept in the context of setting your goals and establishing a strong methodology. To be able to achieve these goals we look at a goal, let's say a 12 month goal. We chunk it down into four quarters. With each quarter we break this down into 13 weeks and then we take a microscope out to look at what we have to do in a week, seven days. This is integral to achieving this goal, hence 4 @13@7.

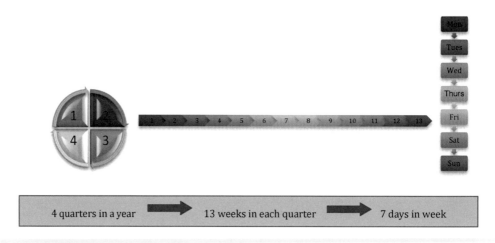

Before we have to chance to do this we need to plan and consider:

"RELAPSE"

It is fair to say that a relapse into your old ways is not failure, it is normal, it is human nature. It is actually so normal, so why don't we actually plan for it?!! Yes I am serious. If we can accept that we will actually not be 100% perfect then we should build in a contingency to take account of the fault that we are actually human. We then have a superb chance of success. I think what I am saying is that having looked at our values, established our goals and mapped out these goals on a vision board, mind map or indeed in a detailed way, we need to actually plan the achievement of the goal.

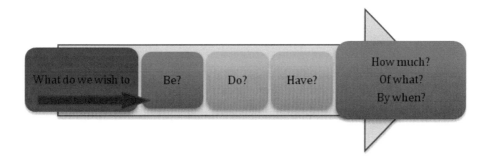

We actually plan our goal by setting down the baby steps and accepting the fact that we have to protect our expectations by creating the consistency to relapse or fail, then to start AGAIN!!!

The key is to <u>RESTART</u>.

Dr A. Grant (2002) created a model which considers relapse and I will consider this with you for a short while. I have created an adaptation of the model a tiny bit for the purposes of this book and I have created my own version to illustrate my meaning.

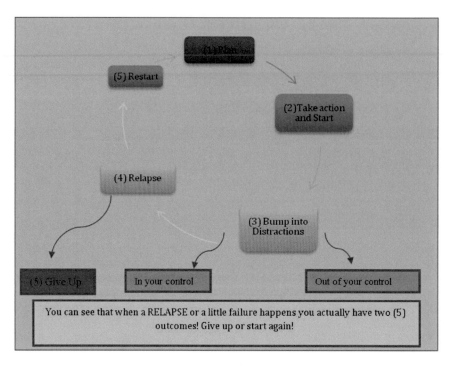

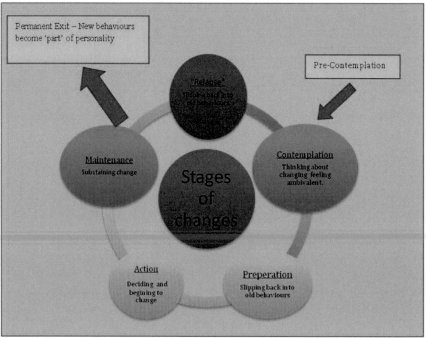

Starting again, getting back on the bicycle is clearly the solution I would advocate; what tools do we have to help us? Well in essence we have an army of helpers we can use to make sure we "get back into the saddle." Plus of course, we have the self awareness highlighted in my first book "*Step and FOCUS*" based on understanding what positive and negative messages are influencing your motivation and behaviour.

We use "the army of helpers" to make sure that the positive thoughts pushing you to restart perusing your goals are at the front of the queue!!!

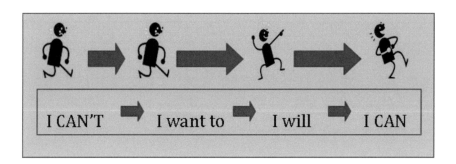

Allow me give you some thoughts or ideas on your army of helpers, to support your goal plan and their successful achievement. Let's look at how we can harness this army to be there to support us and guide us, to help us and to protect us.

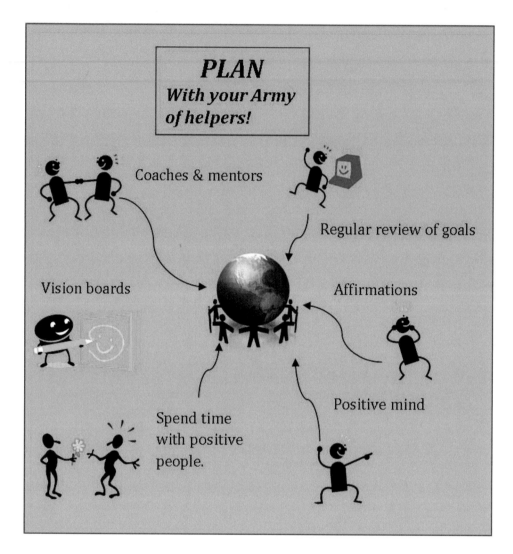

Coaches:

Coaches are all around you? I am in fact one myself and I know how powerful they can be in empowering you towards success. I guess I have had a coach most of my life. Not the same one, a series of them who served me well during different stages of my journey. What will they do for you?

- ➢ *Empower you.*
- ➢ *Challenge you.*
- ➢ *Encourage you.*
- ➢ *Question you.*
- ➢ *Support you.*
- ➢ *Guide you.*

They also underpin your progress with some measure of accountability. They come in all shapes and sizes, covering all walks of life and have all sorts of niche areas of focus. Seek them out, search for the right one and interview them, structure a series of meetings to support you and propel you forward. They will not be *FREE!!!* BUT..... there is great quote I want to share with you:

"Do not count the cost of the shovel when you are digging for gold."

In this case the gold is in you! You need to consider what it is worth to extract the real power within you; to allow you to identify your real potential and then of course, RELEASE IT!!

Mentors:

I think there is some confusion between the terminology between mentors and coaches. My definition is as follows:

> **A Coach – is a specialist in empowerment. He or she does <u>not</u> have to be a specialist in your field or the area of focus. The specialist is in the ability to use human**

understanding to help you understand yourself and move you forward in what you wish to achieve.

A Mentor – has (I hope) all the skills of a coach, but sometimes not. He or she has certainly "been there and done that." What I mean by that is that he or she has achieved success in the way that you wish to achieve success in a given field be it sport, business, life! So they can guide you with quite a lot of "this is what I did."

To seek out a mentor, it is the same process as having a having a coach, or finding a coach. You can have both; they should not however be in conflict. Indeed they may complement each other.

S.T.W.P.P. - Spend. Time. With. Positive. People.

I am pretty certain it was Darren Hardy in his superb book *"The Compound Effect"* (2010), who asked people to go through the following exercise. List all the people you can think of below

Family		Friends		Work Colleagues	
1.					
2					
3.					
4.					
5.					
6.					
7.					
8.					
9.					
10					

OK, now for the hard bit. Put a plus or a minus by each of the names. Be honest, brutally honest. The plus is for the people you deem to be positive, who help you, who support you and who and do not demean you or even (God forbid) bully you. The minus are for the people who are the opposite, now take a great big felt tip pen and cross out all the minus people. What do we have left? We have a positive people pool (P.P.P). They are the people you need and must spend the most of your time with. These are the people you must gravitate towards. Build your days and weeks around this P.P.P and try where possible to avoid the rest – the negative people pool (N.P.P).

Regular Goal Review.

Having spent time, energy and passion establishing and confirming your values and then marrying these to your goals, you have now mapped out your goals based on what you wish to be, have and do. You have gone over the short, medium and long term goals. Wouldn't it be wise to remind yourself what these goals are?!

It doesn't matter if it is daily, weekly, monthly or quarterly, but one thing is for sure whatever you do choose: to make it viable in your busy life, keep it consistent. I review my goals regularly, which for me means twice a month. It does not have to take long. It could be a flick through your goal journal, a review of your mind map or vision board for ten minutes and that's it. What I actually do is do all three, not because I am a "Super Hero," because this sort of thing is my passion. What I do do is sign off the journal, mind map or vision board so that I can check I am actually reviewing them.

What does this review achieve?

> ➢ It keeps the goals alive.
> ➢ It jolts you into action.
> ➢ It nudges your-self accountability.
> ➢ It energises you.
> ➢ It reminds you of what you actually want.

> ➤ It embeds itself into your sub-conscious mind.

Vision boards

I hate newspapers! But the Sunday papers are great and the reason why I love them is that they are packed with magazines, pictures and photos. You can bet your bottom dollar that if you collect three week's worth and then start ploughing through all the photos you will find more than enough material to fill a big collage. Get your scissors and glue out and cut out all the pictures and photos for which to reflect your goals.
Apparently 60% of us interpret the world via our visual sensors so for 6/10 people reading this book, vision boards will be seriously useful. What a lot of people do with their vision boards is to pin it up in their study, pop it on the fridge or put it in a frame in their office.

"Put it anywhere you will see it regularly."

The next step is to look at it as often as you possibly can. It does exactly the same as the goal review, which included the use of the vision boards. It helps bring your goals alive. It serves to create an electro-magnet towards what you wish to achieve. It reminds you possibly daily! What you want, what you are heading for and what you are doing and why you are doing it.

Affirmations

One of my favourite writers Jim Rohn is not keen on affirmations unless they are linked to actions. I agree affirmations on their own are useless.

Affirmations + No action = Dreaming
Affirmations + Action = Momentum

So how do we use affirmations and what are they?

"An affirmation is a statement expressed in the first person expressed out loud and may be used to support or underpin your goals."

I cover this in detail in my first book, *"Step Up and FOCUS."* However, I promise you it works. The affirmations linked to your goals and underpinned with an action plan brain wash you to success.

My five favourite Affirmations

➢ *I smile at challenges, knowing that there is* <u>*always*</u> *a way.*

➢ *I trust the process and I march past every financial battle as a* <u>*victor*</u> *supreme.*

> *My sword (my <u>tenacity</u> and <u>persistence</u>) and my shield (my <u>belief</u> and my <u>confidence</u>) always help me win.*

> *I <u>do</u> <u>not</u> waste time on needless worry I act on challenges "face to face."*

> *I know there is always help at hand, there is always a way.*

Positive Mind Feed (PMF)

This is any form of positive biography, autobiography, success story or personal development book or audio. Where should they sit in your life?? They should become one of your many success habits, you decide on books or audio, I just collect them and get lists from people who chant "you must read x, y and z." I always find out from them why! If I am convinced it goes on to my reading list.

People read at different speeds, so do not set yourself too big a task.

Here are some of the examples of what some of my coaching clients do:

> *10 Minutes (PMF) per day.*
> *10 Pages (PMF) per day.*
> *1 book (PMF) per week.*

> ➢ *1 audio (PMF) per week.*
> ➢ *1 book (PMF) per month.*
> ➢ *1 audio (PMF) per month.*

Whatever the PMF protocol is, it does not matter, but my deep advice to you is to read or listen to something. I tend to read two to three books per month, I have one or two presented in different styles on the go at the same time. I even mind map them, to be able to review and recall them.

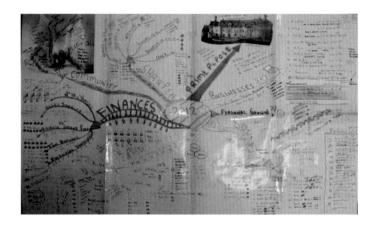

Relapse Story

Graham was an established property investor, a relatively experienced coach in his own right, he was working for a property company freelancing on the sales and marketing side. He had a healthy long term relationship and all was going swimmingly. Over a series of emails it appeared that "nothing was going right," that he wanted to give up coaching and had lost his previously immense passion for property, all in the space of two weeks. I would count that as a relapse!!!!

Overwhelm and panic can happen when you are tired and exhausted. It can happen if multiple "failures" mount up as if they have been waiting to pounce on you. This happened to Graham and it certainly hit him hard just when he least expected it. Thank goodness he had a coach to help him!!!

We did the only thing to do in this type of circumstance; we agreed to take a deep breath. We agreed Graham would take a break from anything he could realistically let go. Graham also deliberately took time out to "review" everything and have a look at the "herd of elephants."

The next thing we did together was to come to an understanding that going through a "relapse" was OK and that it was not a reason for loss of face, embarrassment and definitely not a reason for a loss of confidence. In fact Graham and I talked and talked and realised that what was happening was real progress, because he was pushing at his own boundaries. He was almost bouncing his multiple issues all over the place.

To understand the process of growth, which by definition involves failure and relapse, it stops self-recrimination dead in its tracks. Graham re-found his flow, yes it took three to four weeks, there were a few tears and Graham engaged his whole army of helpers to get him back on track.

What happened here was that Graham went through a massive learning phase and he will not forget it. He stepped out with boldness and achieved the goals that allowed him to live his life with purpose, under his own rules. The reality check is that relapses happen. The fact is that starting again is the only way forward.

Summary

Relapse - where it fits!

        -Expect and anticipate it.

        - Always restart.

Have an army of helpers:

        Coaches and mentors

        Spend time with positive people (S.T.W.P.P)

        Regular goal review

        Vision boards

        Affirmations

        Positive mind feeds (P.M.F)

So....anticipate the relapse, use an army of helpers to get you back on track.

Relapse Affirmations

- ➤ *I am working in the knowledge that things go wrong.*

- ➤ *I am surrounded by an army of helpers to support me.*

- ➤ *I am comfortable and attuned with the fact that I have to have little failures to succeed.*

- ➤ *I am committed to achieving my goals.*

- ➤ *I am focused on surrounding myself with positive people and positive input.*

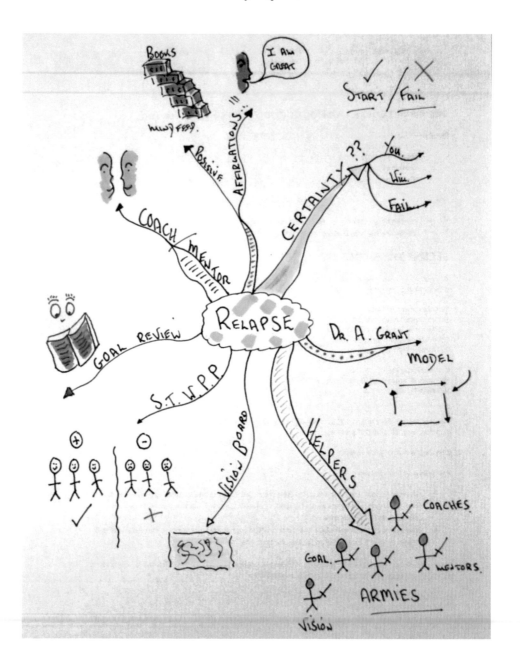

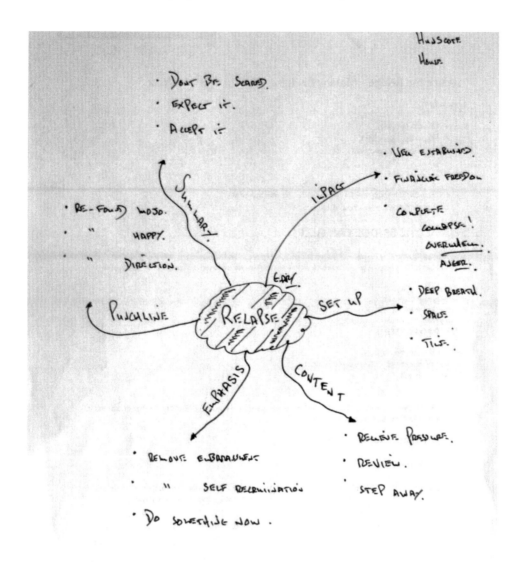

Chapter 4
"4"

"Setting a goal without success markers is like driving on the motorway without sign posts!"

So! We have set out our goals for the next 12 months. We have thrown a harpoon out (mentally) and we have decided what we want to achieve in a variety of different areas of focus in our life. All this, to push us closer to where we wish to be.

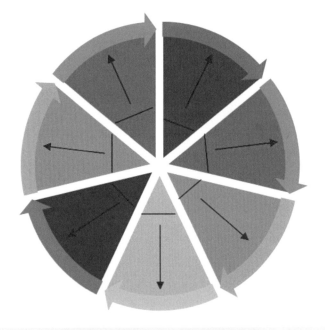

We are not trying to change the world overnight!

We are not taking some Herculean leap to suddenly become perfect.

We are, in a considered way, nudging our way forward to the life we want to have, towards what we wish to be, have and do and in this context create:

➢ Self Accountability.
➢ Clarity.
➢ Success points.
➢ Celebration markers.

We are going to look at the end in mind, the end goal and then, chunk down the goal into "4" easily identifiable road signs or success markers. These logically are the four quarters of the year.

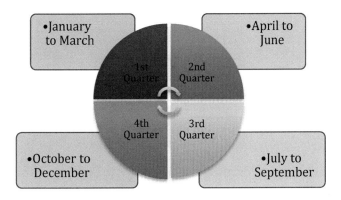

What if we do not do this?

Our intentions may be good, our original motivation may have been strong, but things get in the way and I am all too familiar with people I have worked with who then have an "oops moment." You reach the end of the year. You dust off your goal chart and you realise that whilst you may have started off with the greatest intentions, the goal you nobly set was never completed or fell by the wayside. Yet, what we have built here is 40 chances to reset our new year's resolutions (not that I believe in them, if I am honest!!).

We have easy monitor goals and hard monitor goals and it is worth having a look at these. I have found that a lot of my coaching clients over the years fall foul of not understanding the nuances of defining this element to goal and goal setting.

Easy monitor goals

I do not mean easy goals, by the way. I am referring to goals with very specific measuring points to use as a tool to benchmark, progress and succeed towards achieving a goal. Let's have a look at some examples.

Goal – I am going to lose one stone (14lbs) of weight by the 01.01.2014!

The easy bit is that this goal is easily measured and so if we were to chunk it down to four quarters we could do it one of several ways. We could chunk it down into four equal parts.

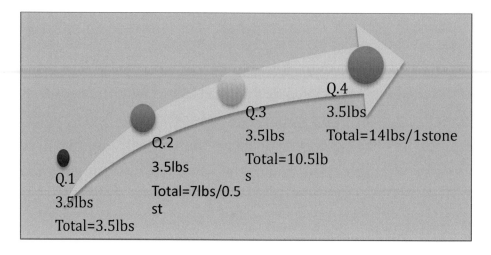

Q.1
3.5lbs
Total=3.5lbs

Q.2
3.5lbs
Total=7lbs/0.5st

Q.3
3.5lbs
Total=10.5lbs

Q.4
3.5lbs
Total=14lbs/1stone

Or live with many challenges, it may be a slow start and then build up to a crescendo at the end. What I mean by that is that in the old days as a sales person we did not break up our year's targets into four equal parts. We broke the year up into 10 parts and assumed an exponential increase as you can see below.

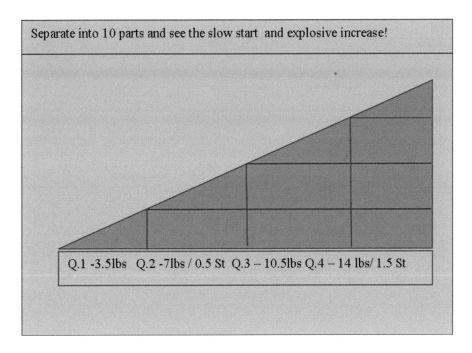

Separate into 10 parts and see the slow start and explosive increase!

Q.1 -3.5lbs   Q.2 -7lbs / 0.5 St   Q.3 – 10.5lbs Q.4 – 14 lbs/ 1.5 St

We do this because of several reasons:

- ➤ Pace of progress.
- ➤ Momentum.
- ➤ Habit formation.
- ➤ Knowledge/understanding/experience.

So you can see we have two potential ways to break down the goals into four quarters and you will have to decide in your own mind which method makes sense to you. This is an appropriate way to work on goals which have an easily monitored quantum (amount) to measure.

Hard monitor (soft) goals

You will have look at your life balance and establish some goals and use what I would call "soft terminology" to describe what you want to achieve. Let me give you some examples:

I am going to do _____more.

I am going to improve _____.

I am going to get better at _____.

I am going to _____faster.

I am going to _____quicker.

Setting these soft goals can on first glance or the less practiced or experienced person can prove a little bit of a challenge. However, in order to achieve a goal we need to have a specific success point, we need to have a quantifiable amount or a figure. So what do we do? We have a look at:

How much more than?

Improve from what to what?

Better than what?

Faster than what?

Quicker than what?

I hope you grasp the idea, let me give you an example. I can take a hard monitor (soft) goal from one of my own goals some years ago.

"I am seeing my sister much <u>more</u> than I used to in 2011."

That was my initial statement, but of course <u>more</u> is just an intention. I needed to ask how much <u>more</u>? More than what? So I took some time to ponder upon what this meant in measurable terms. In this case I looked back at my diary over the past one to two years and indentified that I saw my sister two to three times a year as a general average. So of course the question is then how much more do I wish to see my sister? I decided that I did not wish to take a Herculean jump, why? Well, because we are both busy people. I did decide an improvement would simply be to see my sister at least four times a year. By the way we live in separate towns, have very busy schedules and complicated diaries. So this goal is not as easy as it sounds. How do I chunk it down?

"I am seeing my sister much <u>more</u>, than I used to in 2011."

Q.1	Q.2	Q.3	Q.4
1	2	3	4
Succeeding the goal is seeing my sister four times a year.			

So you can see that even if the goal is on initial scrutiny a hard to monitor goal, with a bit of thought and a little analysis we can find a way to quantify the point we wish to reach. I can assure you this is the case; one common one I come across with individuals is the natural request to improve confidence for example. The process there is quite simple to identify the score of confidence i.e.

In which particular area do you wish to improve your confidence?

Then quite simply ask yourself the questions on a scale of 1/10 or 1/100 where do you regard yourself now and where do you wish to be? Subjective yes, but it is a way to measure success, change and progress!

<u>Let's give this a go!</u>

Choose two of your goals from a previous chapter. Jot down what you wish to achieve over the next year. How much of what by when, what is it you want to be, do, have?

<u>Goal 1</u>

<u>*Goal 2*</u>

Now what we need to do is chunk it down. So take the first goal you have chosen and have a good think. We know where we want to be and what we want to do. So we now do the *"4"* bit in our "4@13@7." Have a look at your goal and break it down into easily recognised success markers towards achieving the main goal.

Where do you need to be at the <u>end</u> of the first quarter in order to achieve the end of the goal? What and where is it reasonable for you to aspire to be? Do the same for the second, third and fourth quarter.

<u>End of the First Quarter</u>

<u>End of the Second Quarter</u>

<u>End of the Third Quarter</u>

<u>End of the Fourth Quarter</u>

Wow! Isn't it great to the goal chunked down?! It looks much easier to digest and achieve if we look at it this way. At the back of the chapter you will see that I have provided you with an example of my *"4"* from *"4*@13@7" for my goal plan in 2012 and also a blank template for you to have ago at.

"Do not forget 'The Rucksack!'"

Some of the goals you would like to work on will be bold, fair and play to you, do not be nervous! You are now working along a structured process which gives you the best possible chance of success. That is what "4@13@7" is about, yet you need to look forward, not back. Remember to let go of your *"Rucksack,"* remember not to dwell on the past issues and failures. Sure, learn from them, but do not carry them with you or they will slow you down. Allow yourself to fly.

"Do not forget 'The Relapse!'"

Look, even though you have laid out your goals things will go wrong, nothing ever goes 100% according to plan. So accept that this will happen, build it into the plan, build it into your mindset.

OK this is what might happen, you have your marker for the end of the first quarter for one of your goals, obviously you review it at the end of the first quarter and you are <u>not</u> quite where you wish to be.

"Do not panic!!!!"

Linking

So, I must confess that I am excited about this whole process:

We have crafted a goal, we have broken it down into four quarters and we have created our own method of accountability. We have, I hope, agreed to allow ourselves some form of recognition or points in our mini quarter goals. We have taken into account *"The Rucksack"* and we have assumed we will *"Relapse!!"*

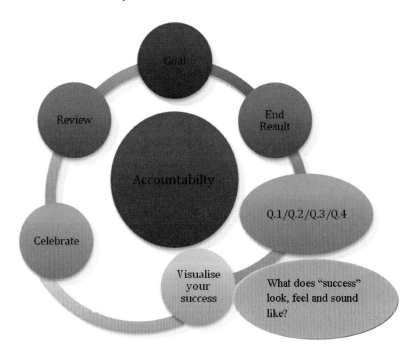

"Story about "4""

Tamsin was a competent, motivated, middle aged woman with all the reasons to succeed. She became involved in a fully comprehensive goal setting process with excitement, passion and energy. The goals were mapped out across the next year. Vision boards were set out for taking ideas and turning them into action, for her goals for the year.

The year pushed on and Tamsin got very, very busy and despite the best laid plans she then realised that the progress towards her goals set at the beginning of the year were no-where near where she wanted them to be. It was May, which is in the middle of quarter, and panic set in. Were all these goals going to be missed? Self doubt and a confidence dive ensued.

Tamsin and I had a good look at the whole situation, we looked at her goals, we looked at the rest of the year. We looked at what was left of Quarter 2 and we looked at Quarters 3 and 4. We then chunked down exactly what needed to be done what action had to be taken.

Tamsin looked at the year and chunked it down based on the fact she still had two full quarters and the bulk of Quarter 2 still to achieve what she wanted. We agreed that with focus, support, friends and a plan, her goals could be achieved with time to spare and time to celebrate.

Tamsin actually achieved the bulk of her goals in the year concerned. Yet that was not the main point of her learning here. The key realisation was that with a goal broken down into four segments things can be achieved.

This was a very different Tamsin than in times past. In the past Tamsin would set out on a goal, things would come in the way. The goal will seem too hard to achieve in the time left. The goal would grow cobwebs and fall to the wayside. Things are a little different now!

Summary

- We have placed "4@13@7" into context.

- We have looked at how to use "4@13@7" in this context.

- We have looked at examples.

- You have tried it out.

- We have looked at examples of how to do it.

- We have reminded ourselves of avoiding *"The Rucksack."* and being aware of the possibility of *"Relapse."*

- At the back of this chapter you can now take action and try the "4@13@7" with eight of your goals.

"4" Affirmations

- *I am focused on using the four quarters strategy.*

- *I am resolute on using the "4@13@7" methodology.*

- *I am positive in the knowledge that I am giving myself the best possible chance to achieve my goals.*

- *I am confident in my plan to complete my goals.*

- *I am using the 4@13@7 strategy to give me 100% focus.*

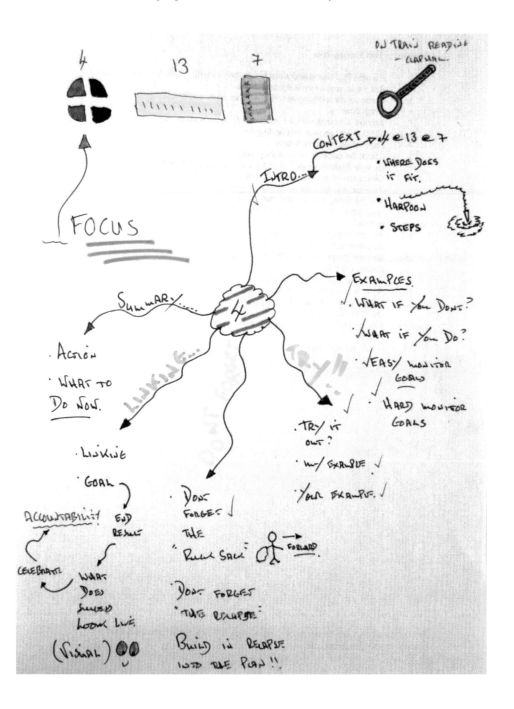

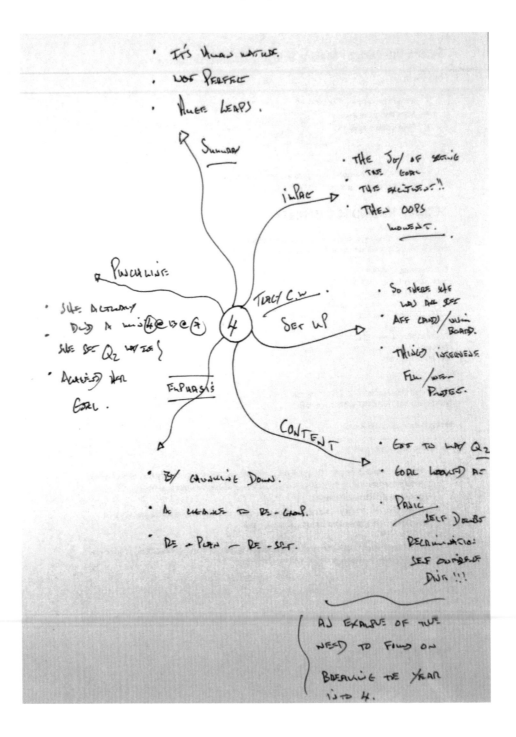

	1st Quarter	2nd Quarter	3rd Quarter	4th Quarter
1	Publish 1st book		Write 2nd book	
2	Swimathon		4 open water swims	
3	Buy- 1	2	3	4 Buy-lets
4	Play guitar 6wk ends	6wkends	6 wkends	6 wkends
5	Take one significant step towards ESE.			
6	Work on grand plan monthly x3	X3	X3	X3
7	Financial statements 3	3	3	3
8	Save 10%	Save 10%	Save 10%	Save 10%

Example of "'4'@13@7" written in 2012

Chunk it down focusing on the 2nd Quarter

	How much of what?	By when?	How?	Helpers?	Celebration
1	Publish 1st book	01/07/12	Via Amazon	GFH S. Searle Smithy	Champagne
2	Swimathon	28/04/12	Training	Tasha/GFH	Pub!
3	Buy1 x BTL	01/07/12	Via the "hopper"	ST and JW	Champagne
4	Plan ESE	01/07/12	Invite "10" venue	MJ, JW and others	New Guitar
5	3 grand plan reviews	01/07/12	Set aside time	Julie bookkeeper	Champagne
6	3 financial statements	01/07/12	⇩	⇩	Chablis
7	Save 10% of everything	01/07/12	Make it automatic	JW	New blazer
8	Play guitar 6/13 wkends	01/07/12	Diarize wkend plan	Me!	New guitar

It is now your turn! What will they look like? Where will you be at the end of ………

Lindsay Hopkins

	1st Quarter	2nd Quarter	3rd Quarter	4th Quarter
1				
2				
3				
4				
5				
6				
7				
8				

Now chunk it down for each quarter! Where do you want to be? What you wish to achieve with your goals? Do this process x 4

	How much of what?	By when?	How?	Helpers?	Celebration
1					
2					
3					
4					
5					
6					
7					
8					

Chapter 5

"13"

"There is little point setting out in a sail ship, without any sails or a motor."

Some people regard 13 as an unlucky number, but for me has always been lucky. Some people may have heard that there is a science called numerology, which helps identify a variety of significant numbers, which have and will feature in one's life, numbers that will also enable and numbers to avoid etc. You will see that the number 13 can be significantly positive for all of us.

We can use 13 to ensure that we can build in contingency and build in *"Relapse;"* we can factor in all the key points converted in the book so far to help us succeed.

Context

We have chunked down our goals to establish what we wish to achieve each quarter, which allows us to look at the goal and monitor success and failure in our journey towards our goals.

"4@13@7"

OK, now let's have a eureka moment! Each quarter has, of course, 13 weeks. Bingo! This is fantastic; we can use this to our advantage in a major way. So it is fascinating we can look at a year in a different way.

Quarter 1	• 13 weeks
Quarter 2	• 13 weeks
Quarter 3	• 13 weeks
Quarter 4	• 13 weeks

So we are now going to peel the onion even further to ensure success. We are now going to put a magnifying glass on each quarter and work out how we can use this magic figure of 13 to our advantage.

Sales

If you read my story you will have seen that I spent a great deal of my life in financial services sales selling – sales managing. The one key to sales of course is to set realistic targets and to achieve them. The same can be true of goals. If we can set a target and then break it down into baby steps, across let's say 13 weeks wouldn't that make sense. It would provide us with a plan, a monitoring process and a way to review progress at a glance. This is exactly what we used to do with sales targets.

What if you do?

What if you do adopt this methodology? It will allow you to do the following:

1. Review progress easily.
2. Identify one step at a time.
3. Create self monitoring and accountability.
4. Adapt to relapse.
5. Build in contingency.

What if you do not?

My goodness, this is not an easy one to answer. We will find that a goal falls away. Our intentions were great when we set the goal but without a "4@13@7" focus, things get in the way. External priorities distract us; take up our lives and our energy away from what we really wish to achieve. We:

"Betray our goals!"

What an awful prospect? Let's just do it and see how magical applying the "4@13@7" methodology works.

Time process

OK so here we go. Just to give you a feel and a sense of how I used to apply the 13 week rule back in my sales days. We simply did the following; we set a target (goal). We then broke it down into ten weeks <u>only</u>. So the target was set to be done in ten weeks. I can sense you are thinking "what about the other three weeks?" Well we used to joke about this and allocate one week to have flu! One week to deal with a family crisis! and one week to have a holiday or celebrate. Bizarre but if you think about it, we automatically build in a contingency or we accounted for slippage or a *"Relapse,"* brilliant!!

So let me show you what it looked like. Let's assume I had a target of 80 sales (it does not matter what type of sales). That, in theory eight per week over ten weeks, so our plan would look like this:

Week	Sales
1	8
2	8
3	8
4	8
5	Flu
6	8
7	8
8	8
9	8
10	Family crisis
11	8
12	8
13	Holiday

Some might think this is very whacky! But I can assure you that doing the 10/13 method each quarter meant our sales results were pretty focused. The clue here is that we can apply this same focus to our goals. We can take our quarter goals, which have been mapped out and so we now take one of our quarter goals and have a look at an example of how we apply the 10/13 plan.

I train to do some long distance swims from time to time and so my goal in 2012 was to swim 5000m in April 2012 so in the first quarter I had to get up to speed. I mapped it out like this and I can share with you what happened.

Week	Distance Target	Actual distance
1	600m x3	600m x3 ✅
2	600m x3	600m x2
3	800m x3	800m x3 ✅
4	1000m x3	1000m x3 ✅
5	1000m x3	Flu!!
6	Crisis/"Relapse"	1000mx3 ✅
7	1500m x3	1500m x3 ✅
8	1500m x3	1500m x3 ✅
9	Flu!!	Bad back!!
10	2000m x3	2000m x2
11	2500m x3	2500m x3 ✅
12	3000m x3	2500m x1
13	Rest	2500m x3 ✅

I chunked it down based on advice, I built in a chance to *"Relapse"* as a contingency because things happen. We get distracted. In my case I had a bad back and flu. It did not go exactly to plan but nothing ever does. However I was ready, I was swim fit, I raised some money for charity and did my personal best! It was not perfect, but nothing ever is. It did, on the other hand, work!

This is how to chunk down a quarter goal and then take a weekly plan and impose a plan into my life to make the goal come alive and grow legs.

Now it is your turn! Have a look at one of your goals. Have a look at the chunked down quarterly goal and now have a go at "4@'**13**'@7":

So here it goes:

Annual Goal

How much of what by when?

First quarter goal

Don't forget:

Add in your *"Relapse"*!!

Add in your contingency!!

Allow yourself to be human!!

Week	What do you need to do?	What have you actually done?
1		
2		
3		
4		
5		
6		
7		
8		
9		
10		
11		
12		
13		

Top Ten Tips

The top 10 tips I have for you in order to craft your "4@**13**@7" plan and run it effectively:

No1: Take your time over the planning.
Find a quiet place, honour yourself by giving you time.

No2: Do not try to do too much. Do not overstretch.
Do not set yourself too high a target which is destined to fail.

No3: Consider the four quarters first and look at the whole picture.
So put the 10/13 plan into the context of the year plan.

105

No4: You <u>must</u> structure the goal and action targets over ten weeks only.

You build in something similar to the flu, crisis, and holiday plan.

No5: Structure and build in a <u>celebration</u> at the end or at logical points over the 13 weeks.

There will be logical points where you can be proud of achievements.

No6: Consider <u>escalating</u> activity and actions to watch increased confidence and mental or physical fitness through the 13 weeks.

We all improve and get better so plan accordingly and logically.

No7: Work out a system to <u>monitor</u> and <u>review</u> your progress.

Some form of constant regular reminder of the task is needed.

No8: share your plans with a positive close circle of people.

By declaring intentions to others you enlarge help and affirm out loud.

No9: Be prepared to adapt and redraft the plan.

Nothing ever goes according to plan and so be accepting of this.

No10: Do not give up!

You set the goal based on what you really want, so why give up?

It is worth looking at top ten tips No7. Once we have a plan in place there is no point sitting the folder or worksheet and leaving it. You will forget you will be distracted; you will be dragged away from your focus. You need to create a way to make the 10/13 plan accessible and obvious. Here are some ideas:

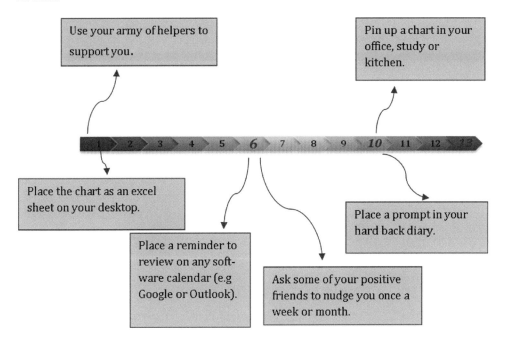

You will see at the back of this chapter an example of how I broke down 10/13 plan in Quarter 2 of 2012. I have also given you a template to fill in your 10/13 plan. When I have been out doing workshops, seminars and network meeting talks going through "4@13@7" concepts I have been asked to share what these mean, just to help people truly understand how to apply these methods. So have a flick through the back of the chapter. I will explain the basics and rationale of each of the three of the eight goals across the second quarter of 2012. I hope this helps give you a feel of how to play the game, of how you can put muscle and focus behind your aspirations, your crafted goals.

> No1: My goal here in 2012 was to publish my first book "Step Up and FOCUS." At this stage the writing had been done, but in this quarter I needed to work with the editor who was setting up the structure and layout of the books. So, in order to make sure that this stayed in focus and the project kept moving. My action was identified as, the need for one call or emails a week to the editor. In reality I would have been happy with 10/13 prompts or updates with the editor. I monitored this as described, and the book was ready to go to print on the 1st July 2012. BINGO!

> No2: This was a fitness and charity goal swimming 5000 metres in an indoor pool on the 26/04/12. It was for a charity called *Make a Wish Foundation* so in the context of the second quarter of 2012, I only had four weeks to train left and then the swim. The objective was to swim every day i.e. 26 days in April up to the event. This was one third of the 13 week plan and to plan for relapse or failure and interruption I decided I would be happy with 20/26 days swimming as a success measure. With this I kept the monitoring very simple. I grabbed a pile of post-it notes numbered them 26 to 0 then each day I did a swim I put a great big tick across the post-it.

> *"I actually managed 22/26 and I really did get in the mood with this goal."*

No3: this was a property purchase goal for 2012, which was to buy four properties in South Wales over the course of 2012. The way I knew this would or could stand the most chance of happening was to make sure that I visited South Wales once a month. The way I made this happen was to plan my diary and ensure that in April, May and June 2012 I actually did the visits. The key to ultimately achieving this goal within this quarter was to be honest, making the decision. Understanding that if the diary was locked out and as long as either I or my P.A. did not change the diary then these visits would happen. I lead a busy life and every day is valuable and precious but so is my property goal in terms of wealth creation. So, surprise, surprise it actually happened. In reality in terms of slippage and *"Relapse"* success would have been 2/3 visits in the quarter, but I actually did 3/3.

So you can see that you do have to apply the top ten tips to your "4@13@7" plan. You have to adapt it to your life and you have to craft your life <u>around</u> what actions have to be taken in accordance with your goal plan. Is this too analytical? Actually I would contest not. Business is built around structure, processes and protocols. So, all that we are doing is working on ourselves as <u>our</u> business.

Is this easy? No! It is hard work, however the reality is that if these beautiful goals you have crafted are in total synergy to your values, we need to honour what you really wish to do and to be and have with a proper realistic plan!!

Story of "13"

I worked with a tremendous character as a sales manager and the character was called Ben. He flexed his muscles at the start of one of the quarters one year and emerged with a statement of pretty huge sales target for the quarter. Even I thought it was a little bit of a stretch, but he asked me to help him.

Ben and I chunked down the target the way I had been taught. We planned the target (sales goal) over ten weeks not 13. We allowed for flu, family crisis and even a week to celebrate and have time off. We even planned a review at the end of each week and an action plan for the following week, off Ben went with impressive energy and commitment.

The quarter started superbly and Ben was forging ahead and was "walking on water," then relative (sales) disaster struck, his mother became ill. He had to take time out and went through some incredible emotional turmoil at the bedside of his mother in hospital. Happily she recovered.

So Ben returned to his sales target at the end of week eight out of 13, with four weeks to go and a tough target to achieve. The superb thing was we had a three week contingency. It may be that this sounds like a fairy story, but Ben went on and smashed his sales target goal.
Ben clearly went through a lot of heartache and many pride issues. We worked in a harsh sales environment where once the senior sales member opened their mouth with a target it had to be done "irrespective."

By the application of planning a quarter and chunking it down into 13 weeks and building in the chance for "blips," Ben had given himself the best possible chance of success. The two week disruption was severe and painful but recovery and success was indeed possible because we had planned for it already.

Summary

- 13 is <u>not</u> un-lucky.

- It allows contingency and "Relapse."

- Context in the "4@13@7" plan.

- Saves targets and goal targets.

- How to lay out your 13 week plan.

- Top 10 tips to doing your 13 week plan.

- Examples of my own.

"13" Affirmations

- I am focused on managing each quarter well.

- I am planning each 13 weeks cycle with passion.

- I am planning each 13 week cycle with a reality focus.

- I am planning each 13 week cycle with baby success steps.

- I am working through each quarter with enthusiasm.

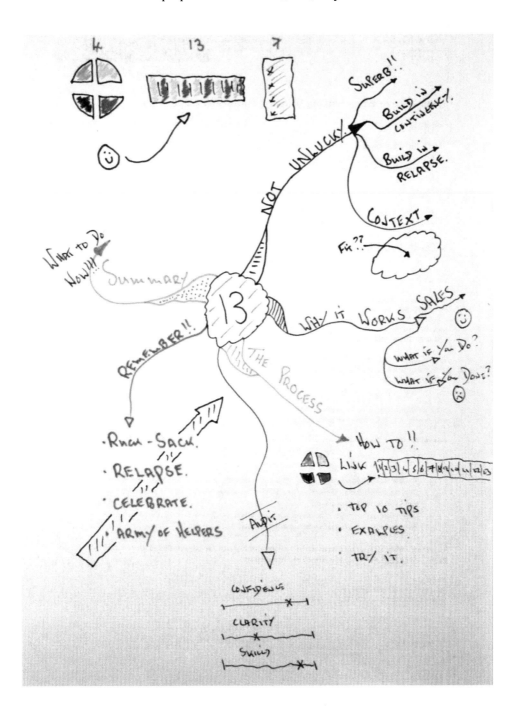

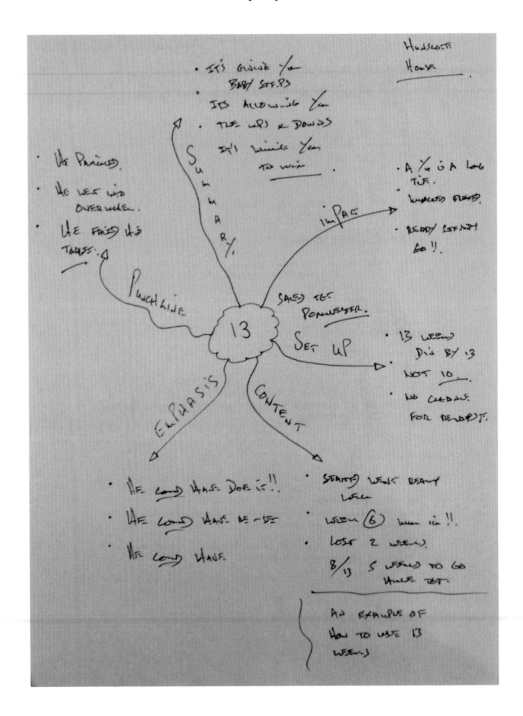

Let's look at Quarter 2.......
What do we have to do each week to a make it happen?
PLAN to do it in ten weeks. NOT 13!!!

	Goal	What I must do!	1	2	3	4	5	6	7	8	9	10	11	12	13
1	Publish 1st book	Push S.Searle Weekly	☺							→					→
2	Swimathon 28/04	Train every day (Where ever poss.)	☺	☺	☺	☺		Rest of quarter plan Open water →							
3	Buy 4 homes	Monthly visit to Wales			☺							☺			
4	Monthly £ management	Instruct Julie			☺							☺			
5	Apply 10% Rule	Contract with JW automatic 105	☺									→			
6	Play more guitar	Play 6x (30 mins)	☺		☺			☺		☺		☺			☺
7	Work on grand plan	Monthly review			☺					☺			☺		
8	E.S.E	Decide on action													☺

You are now going to try it yourself ....
Remember plan to do it in ten weeks. NOT 13!!!

	Goal	What I must do!	1	2	3	4	5	6	7	8	9	10	11	12	13
1															
2															
3															
4															
5															
6															
7															
8															

I have also added the two other charts mentioned in this chapter again so you can see your goals in one go and really crack "4@13@7."

Annual Goal

How much of what by when?

First quarter goal

Week	What do you need to do?	What have you actually done?
1		
2		
3		
4		
5		
6		
7		
8		
9		
10		
11		
12		
13		

We need to honour what you really wish to do, be, have with a proper realistic plan!!

Chapter 6
"7"

"A wasted day, leads to a wasted week, month, year and the next thing you know it…..there is one life gone."

We have crafted our goals which are in synergy with our values. We have broken them down into chunks. We have a goal and then four mini goals to match the four quarters of the year. We have then taken a magnifying glass and broken down each quarter into 13 weeks and looked at plans to take into account relapse and crisis, as well as the chance to celebrate. We have put muscle and process into the goals. We have made them come alive!! A very long way from an initial idle intention or a wish!!

Now we are going to take the last vital step in the "4@13@7" process.

We are going to look at how we make sure the quarterly goals and the 13 week plan can be transported into our weekly lives. You see one week is a chunk of our life: 2% of your year, 7.69% of each quarter. It is not, in my view, to be squandered. As some people reading this book will know from my first book "Step Up and FOCUS," I am a great proponent of setting up solid, healthy, success habits. The need therefore to value time is definitely part of these habits. Perhaps you might need to consider are you a time squanderer or a time cherisher? Are you time aware? Or does time just play tricks with your day and you "never know where the day had gone?" There are ways to overcome these issues if indeed you have come out with an answer you don't like!!

It is interesting as we all have such different lives and circumstances: single, married, young children, old children so it's very different to take a "template to fit all" with how to look at your day. Nonetheless, if you bare with me and we look at what might be a typical day for one or two people who I have worked with and coached, I believe we can plan out some key things which will help us to apply the –

$$\boxed{\text{"4@13@\underline{7}"}}$$

It is by dissecting things to this extent we can actually see how we can turn bold goals into true goals which can be achieved. I appreciate this may not match your life exactly but perhaps have a go at these questions.

Get up & start your day.	• 1. What time do you wake up? • 2. What time do you leave you home?
Travel to work	• 3. What is your journey time to work? = _____ hrs.
Work	• 4 .What time are your working hours to?_____ = _____ hrs.
Lunch	• 5. Do you work through or take a break, if so how long?_____.
Work	• 6.Are you able, allowed to make phone calls, send personal emails at work? Yes/No
Travel home	• 7. What is your journey time home? = _____ hrs. _____.
Early evening	• 8.What time do you eat?_____. • 9. Who do you eat with?_____.
Late evening	• 10. Do you just collapse and watch TV? Yes/No
Sleep	• 11. What time do you go to sleep? • 12. How many hours a night do you sleep? = _____ hrs.

You might be thinking "oh my goodness," this is a little intrusive asking all these questions, but what we want to have a look at is the whoosh problem. There you are waking up at, let's say, 7:00am Monday morning and before you know it, it is bedtime Friday. That is what I call a whoooosh problem!!

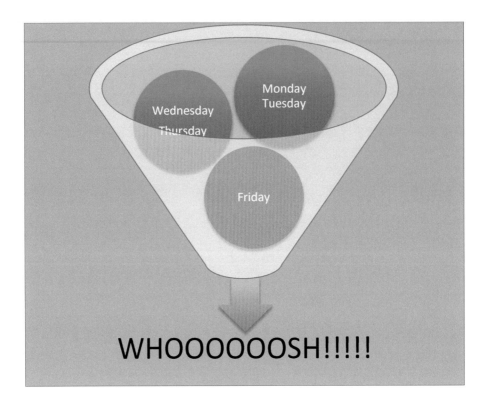

WHOOOOOOSH!!!!!

No time for anything let alone doing anything about achieving some progress in your goals. By placing an x-ray on your week we may be able to find some ways to prevent this happening. So let us look back at the little analysis you did on the day.

Wake up

Let's look at wake up time. Too simplistic I know but I see people or hear of people being larks or owls. Larks are early risers and like to go to bed early, owls are the opposite, bed late up late! Sadly if you are working <u>for</u> someone they may not provide you with a contract that conforms to what suits you!! So to be fair as a lark I would say that the advice I am issuing here for larks could simple be applied at the end of the day by owls! The key point is can we possibly start our day well and is there time or could we make time to add in some goal time? Let me give you some examples of what I have seen some of my coaching clients do.

Example 1: Reading

One of my clients loved the concept of reading positive mind feed and self help books, yet never had time! But was quite prepared to spend ten minutes in the morning drinking a cup of tea and watching negative mind feed on the TV. One of her goals was to read more. More than what? More than one book a year, month, week? Well, in truth the effect of adding ten minutes reading per day into her life was significant (assuming that she can read, let's say, 10 pages a day).

=30 x 10 pages per month

= 300 pages per month = 1 book roughly.

Well unless I am very much mistaken that by being time aware thus "grabbing back" ten minutes of her life she went from one book a year to reading 12. Goal achieved.

Example 2: Fitness

Many of my clients discover this one!! The art of setting up the alarm for 20 to 30 minutes earlier each day with the plan on going for a run, following an exercise regime, going to the gym or going cycling. It is not that simple I know. The temptation to press the snooze button on the alarm is very strong I am sure. Equally if the why is there and really strong enough the body will guide you out of bed. The point is that the "I wish I had time" comment fails upon your own stony ground, against a spotlight of your own desire to craft your own life, your way!!

I am lucky, I am a lark. I decided in July 2012 to swim every day and that is what I do. It works for me on all fronts and very much reflects back to my first book *"Step up and FOCUS"* where I am guiding and encouraging people to have a protocol to start their day to be "the best that they can be." The lucky bit is that I have learned the 21 days habit game. So I knew that if I swam for 21 days in a row, a habit would be formed and the rest of the goal would be a breeze. Goal - swim 70 days out of 91 (a 13 week cycle and one quarter of the year). I did this with ease, goal achieved. So far I have seen so many people do this as well.

Travel to work

The use of travel time, or should I say the misuse, is widely covered by a large number of writers. Suffice to say however, an example of time usage here is worth covering. Let's say travel to work and back each day were 30 minutes each way, so that is an hour a day, indeed five hours a week, 260 hours a year. This is time to do something! If one of your goals is to be, have or do something I would imagine that this might involve learning a new skill or increasing your existing skill to a higher level. Well there we have it! Below is an example for you to create on your own.

Fill in the gaps:

Travel time to work = _____mins.

Travel time home = _____min.

= _____mins/days.

x 5 days = _____mins/p-week.

x 52 days a year _____mins/p-year.

When I work with people, sometimes we work out the figure involved it can be staggering. An hour each way, ten hours a week, 520 hours a year that is a 65 hour (eight-hour day) course of some sort. If you cannot read you listen (audio). One thing is for sure if you have a goal to learn something you have just found another solution to time starvation or the whoosh problem!!

I think you are beginning to see where I come from within the "4@13@7" process. At the weekly level we think we have little or no time, with application and chance we find that we do!! I am now sure that you will see from the answers you gave from your day plan analysis we have time, we make time. In *"Step Up and FOCUS"* I covered how you plan your weekend, you vary your weekend and you even compartmentalise your weekend, to ensure that you have <u>time</u> to work on your goals. Have a look at this example:

		Saturday	*Sunday*
7:00	Early A.M	Swim 30 mins	Swim 30 mins
8:00			
9:00			
10:00			
11:00	Late A.M		
12:00			
13:00		Lunch	
14:00	Early P.M	Play Guitar either day for 30 mins	
15:00			
16:00			
17:00	Afternoon	Read 30 mins	Read 30 mins
18:00			
19:00	Evening		
20:00	Late		
21:00	Evening		

This individual (me!) wanted to swim every day, play guitar once a weekend, read 30 minutes a day, and have quality adventures with the family. Have a look at the gaps filled here. It is not hard, it is just a bit of planning. At the back of the chapter I have copied one of my weekend plans to show you how I do.

In the example above out of 16 waking hours a day x2 = 32, I have grabbed back two half-hours of my weekend to be able to create progress in three goal areas, which leaves 13 half-hours for a family adventure!!

At the back of this chapter I have also given you a detailed example of how the quarterly goals have then been chunked down into 13 week chunks and then positioned on to a week. This is how to create your "4@13@7." Before you have a look what steps could you take to prevent a "whoosh" week, bearing in mind your goals, what five steps could you take?

1. I can_____.
2. I will_____.
3. I will_____.
4. I can _____.
5. I will _____.

In addition, have a look at your weekend, what could you do to add back into your weekend the application of your goal plans? Scribble in some ideas.
What time can you grab back for you??

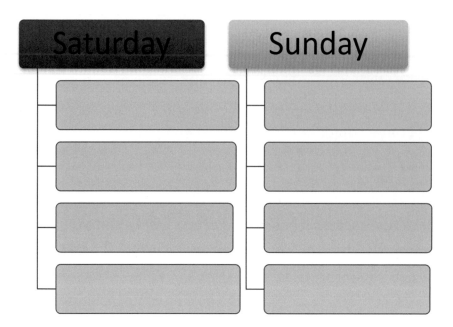

Story about "7"

A week is a long time, seven days, and in fact if we allow for eight hours sleep it is actually 112 waking hours a week. Jennifer was well aware of this and one of her goals for the year was to adopt the habit of reading positive mind feed and self improvement books at a high volume. In fact she had twenty six books piled up by her bedside table ready to read.

Not only did Jennifer have 26 books but we reached a point where she was being teased by her husband. We reached a point where despite the quarterly goals and 13 week plan, the reading was not happening and this was really getting her down. It was eating away at her confidence.

Jennifer and I agreed to look at things at a micro level. By that I mean we had to look at actually what happened to the 112 waking hours of each week. How was it that despite the fact that the goal was clear and "the why" was strong enough, progress was not happening! In fact no reading was happening at all.

Jennifer and I looked at her dairy to attempt to find some way to allow this goal to be infiltrated into her life, her day and her busy week. It is always my clients who come up with the answers, never me. This was true yet again in this case.

The eureka moment came when we realised that Jennifer spent an one hour getting to work and one hour getting back each day. What she used to do was simply listen to the news on the radio. We replaced the books by doing a swap for audio books. Suddenly we had five days of two hours a day as Jennifer's mobile audio university.

This story is very similar to a great number of coaching clients I work with. By looking in depth at the seven day picture and seeing where some time for Jennifer's goals could belong, her frustration and loss of confidence and teasing from her husband fell away.

Summary

- The context of "7" is "4@13@7".

- Why a week is important.

- Are you time aware? Do you squander or cherish your week?

- What does your day look like?

- What does you week look like?

- What does your weekend look like?

- Imposing "4@13" on your "7" day week.

"7" Affirmations

- I am embedding my goal actions into every week.

- I am using all my imagination to make my goals come alive.

- I am creatively crafting my goals into my weekly plan.

- I am respecting the fact that a week should be cherished.

- I am applying the "4@13@7" plan into my week to achieve superb results.

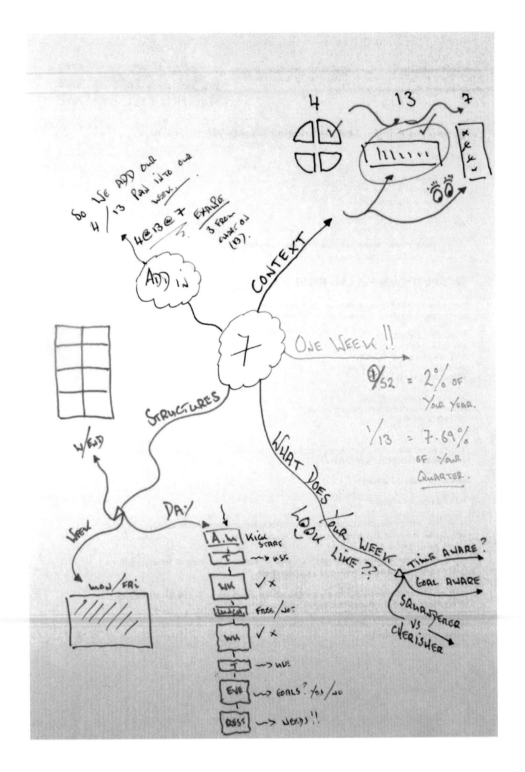

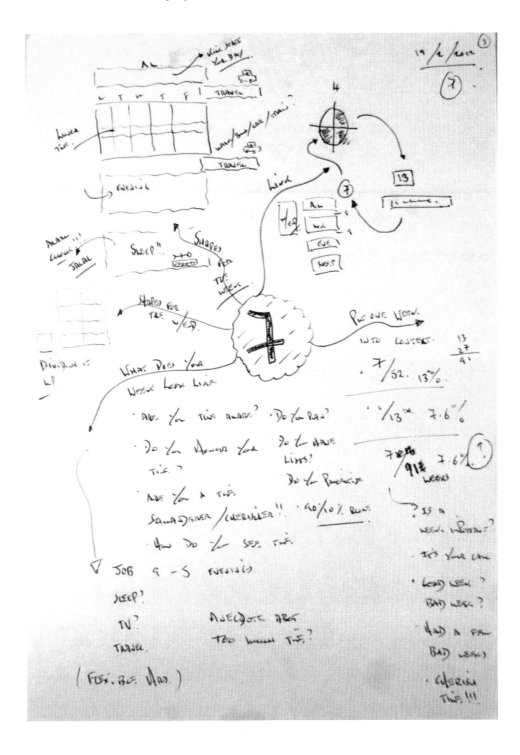

What has to happen each week to move your goal forward?

Is it something every day? Once a week?

I find it easier to separate my week and my weekend up as follows checking as I go along each week.

		Monday	Tuesday	Wednesday	Thursday	Friday	Quick wkly Check list
Before you start work	06:00						
	07:00	Swim	Swim	Swim	Swim	Swim	Swim every day
On the way	08:00	Read	Read	Read	Read	Read	= fitness goal
A.M. At Work	09:00	W	W	V	W	Personal	Time with family
	10:00	O	O	I	O	Finance	= family goal
	11:00	R	R	S	R	meeting	
	12:00	K	K	I	K		
Lunch	13:00			T			
P.M. At Work	14:00	W	W		W	W	
	15:00	O	O	W	O	O	
	16:00	R	R	A	R	R	
	17:00	K	K	L	K	K	
Way Home	18:00			E			
Early Evening	19:00			S			
	20:00	Time	Date		Time	Dinner	
Late Evening	21:00	With	With	Night	With	With	
	22:00	Daughter	Wife	In	Son	Friends	
	23:00	BED	BED	Wales	BED	BED	

		Saturday	Sunday	Quick Weekend Check
Early morning	06:00			
	07:00	Swim & Read	Swim& read	1. Swim x2
Mid Morning	08:00			2. Write book
	09:00	Call Dad	Call Mum	3. Play guitar
Late morning	10:00		Own	4. Wife adventure
	11:00	Chores	Time	5. Call Dad
	12:00		Fun	6. Call Mum
Lunch	13:00	Family Meal		7. Family time
	14:00			8. Review week
Early After-noon	15:00		Adventure with	9. Plan Week
	16:00	60 mins Book	Mrs Hopkins	10. Review Goals
Afternoon	17:00	Writing		11. Affirmations
	18:00		Play Guitar	
Early Evening	19:00	Relax or	Plan week	
	20:00	Social or	Review week	
	21:00	Out for dinner		
Late Evening	22:00	etc		
	23:00			

It is now your turn. You could photocopy one of these off for each week with your goal break down.

This can then be done for each quarter and put up on a board where you will see it everyday and have a copy in your wallet or diary too. You then have your "4@13@7."

		Monday	Tuesday	Wednesday	Thursday	Friday	Quick Wkly Check list
Before you start work	06:00						
	07:00						
On the way	08:00						
	09:00						
A.M. At Work	10:00						
	11:00						
	12:00						
Lunch	13:00						
P.M. At Work	14:00						
	15:00						
	16:00						
	17:00						
Way Home	18:00						
	19:00						
Early Evening	20:00						
	21:00						
Late Evening	22:00						
	23:00						

		Saturday	Sunday	Quick Weekend Check
Early morning	06:00			
	07:00			
Mid Morning	08:00			
	09:00			
Late morning	10:00			
	11:00			
	12:00			
Lunch	13:00			
	14:00			
Early Afternoon	15:00			
	16:00			
Afternoon	17:00			
	18:00			
Early Evening	19:00			
	20:00			
	21:00			
Late Evening	22:00			
	23:00			

<u>Conclusion</u>

My goal in this book was to expose another layer of managing goals and ensuring the best possible chance of them being achieved. I have given you another peek into my mindset and my world. Showing you a series of steps "4@13@7" which are another way in which I successfully achieve my "success habits" or "handrails of success." They have assisted me in achieving my goals, one of those being my second book. I have shared with you once more the tools used in different areas which I have tried out, modified and then adopted as part of my life. For me it is a natural evolution for you to now be the best you can be, living life, your life, with intention and focus. I hope you find it fun "Stepping Up and Focusing" but it will be hard work.

The first step was to understand yourself. To gain full self-awareness on how you communicate, learn and what your strengths and weaknesses are. This will have led to you naturally identifying your true core values, thus establishing your goals with a regular review process. This first step is a giant step and one that some people never take. However, beyond this is the need to manage and monitor and adjust these goals as you go through your journey.

You will need to apply yourself and fuse yourself to your goals. You may try a few things and then forget and so the key is to stick to "4@13@7." If you forget, get distracted, have a family emergency, are ill, just remember it is just a relapse, you have already planned for it. Don't panic! Simply try again!

I have shared with you once more my story since the age of 23 and the advice I would give the 23-year-old knowing what I know now, and a year on from *"Step Up and Focus"* I have also shared with you ten more success habits that I have found to be vital for me and I hope these will be useful to you. Beyond this is the need to manage and monitor and adjust these goals as you go through your journey.

If you are striving to be successful, whatever that may mean to you, you must accept that it is necessary to maintain a continuous state of alertness and active review of your progress and continually refine the tools and success habits to help you move forward.

I have presented you with what I see as the natural stages of creating the building blocks to your accelerated performance. All you need to do now is implement some or all of them!

If you want stronger guidance from a professional you may even want to look at my web site www.futureperformancecoaching.com and enlist my help or the help of my team of superb coaches on a programme of face-to-face coaching, phone coaching or a mixture of the two. Or indeed you may simply email me personally (lindsay@trafalgarsq.co.uk) and be placed on an alert list for when I am running a workshop or seminar and come and meet me which would be a delight, indeed!

I am on what is known as the "property network circuit" in the UK which is, as you now know, where I first started on the coaching journey that I am still on. So if you search for your local property network meeting in your town or city I am bound to turn up and meet you at some stage soon.

You will also see that I produce a series of affirmation CDs which are based on helping you kick-start the day and help with your "daily set up." The feedback I get from these CDs is that they really do help, so you may wish to try one out.

Whatever happens enjoy the "step up" and enjoy the thrill and pure adrenalin rush involved when you:

First – Step Up

Then - F.O.C.U.S – Follow One Course Until Successful.

Lastly - Chunk it all down into "4@13@7" – 4 quarters, 13 weeks in a quarter, 7 days in your week.

What *Now*?

Well done, you have finished reading my second book. I always feel one more little step closer to understanding the way the world works every time I finish another positive mind feed book.

It is timely as I finished writing this book between Christmas and New Year 2012. This is exactly the time of year when I sit down and craft my goals, so I have included copies of my "4@13@7" plan for the annual goals I had for 2012. Some bits are written in my own code but I trust you will "get" my thought process. Based on your eight goals for this year why don't you have a go crafting your "4@13@7" plan for the next quarter? I promise you it is fun and it works! This is why I have included blank sets of templates for you to give it a go yourself, to put your own thought process on it, add pictures, colour and put you into "4@13@7."

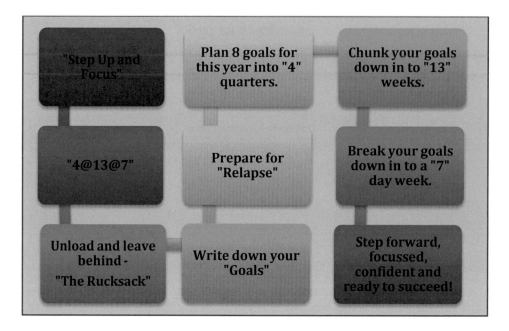

In *"Step Up and FOCUS"* I mentioned that when I read a personal development book I tend to do so "actively" and take the following approach:-

> ➢ I speed read the book or skim through it at outset.

> ➢ I sign and date the front of the book to take "ownership."

> ➢ I use sticky notes and highlighter pens to mark key points that I deem important.

> ➢ I also keep a book journal which I use as a reference book and I mind map the book.

A few pages from my book journal.

NOW WHAT?

I believe you have some questions to ask or decisions to make:

1. Shall I use some of the information and try some of the ideas outlined in this book to help me?

2. Great read but I shall do nothing with this information!

3. Great read and I will come back to it one day!

Any of the three decisions is fine with me, it's your life! But if your decision is No. 1, then my advice is to spend 20/30 minutes and take this time to decide how much, of what, and by when, will you apply this knowledge.

You may wish to engage a friend or buddy to help you with this and to call you to prompt you every couple of weeks and ask you how it's going, calling you to account.

I understand that a self-help book, a positive mind feed book or a personal development book will help simply by reading it and doing nothing. The message will be retained in your subconscious and you will apply some of the ideas, of that I am sure!

However, as my daughter commented "But if I really want to use this book properly, what shall I do now?" So if you wish to take decision No. 1, you need to map out your "4@13@7" to weave this learning into your life, to help you improve and move towards successfully achieving your goals faster. I have made this step easier for you!

I have included each step for you. All the resources you need are at the back of each chapter, first "4" then "13" and lastly "7."

Recommended Reading and Reference points

By Author, Year, Title, Publisher

Adams. Scott, 2002, *Another Day in Cubic Paradise*, Dilbert

Adewale. Micheal, 2008, *Class Dismissed*, Micheal Adewale

Aldows, Hugh, 1983, *How to set up & run your own business*, Daily Telegraph

Austin-Smith, A, 2013, *Fantastic: When being good is not enough*, Capstone Publishing Ltd.

Bamford, Martin , 2006, *The Money Tree*, Pearson

Blanchard, K; Bowles, S, 1998, *Gung Ho!*, Harper Collins

Blanchard, K; Bowles, S, 1998, *Raving Fans!*, Harper Collins

Blanchard; Zigarmi; Zigarmi, 1985, *Leadership & the One Minute Manager*, Fontana/Collins

Bono, Edward. de , 1971, *Lateral Thinking of Management*, Penguin

Bono, Edward. de, 1985, *Six Thinking Hats,* Penguin

Bono, Edward. de, 1985, *Tactics*, Fontana

Borg, James, 2004, *Persuasion*, Pearson

Breithaupt, Tim, 1999, *10 Steps to Sales Success,* Amacom

Buchrach, Bill, 2000, *Values-Based Financial Planning,* Aim High

Buzan, Tony, 1971, *The Speed Reading Book*, BBC

Buzan, Tony, 2001, *Head Strong,* Thorsons

Canfield; Hansen; Hewitt, 2000, *The Power of Focus*, Vermillion

Carlon, Richard, 2002, *What About the Big Stuff,* Positive

Chapman, G; Campbell, R, 2005, *The Five Love Languages of Children,* Northfield Publishing

Chapman, Gary, 2010, *The 5 Love Languages,* Northfield Publishing

Clayton, Mike, 2011, *Brilliant Stress Management*, Pearson

Collins, Jim, 2009, *How to the Mighty Fall and Why Some Companies Never Give In,* Ransom House

Cope, Mike, 2010, *The Secrets of Success in Coaching* , Pearson

Davidson, Jeff, 2000, *Project Management*, Alpha

Ditzler, Jinny, 1994, *Your Best Year Yet*, Thorsons

Dr Batra, Ravi, 1988, *The Great Depression of 1990*, Bantam

Dr Briers, Stephen, 2009, *Brilliant Cognitive Behavioural Therapy*, Pearson

Dr Kashel, Gerald, 1984, *The 4%*, Sidgwick & Jackson

Dr Miller, Liz, 2009, *Mood Mapping*, Rodale

Eysenck, H; Wilson, G, 1975, *Know Your Own Personality*, Book Club Associates

Farell, Dominic, 2006, *The Jet-to-Let Bible*, Lawpack

Ferguson, Marc, 1995, *Sales Esteem*, Pax

Ferriss, Timothy, 2007, *The 4-Hour Week*, Vermillion

Freemantle, David, 2004, *The Buzz*, Nicholas Brealey

Gallo, Carmine, 2010, *The Presentation Secrets of Steve Jobs,* McGraw-Hill

Gerber, Michael. E, 1995, *The E Myth*, Harper Collins

Gitomer, Jeffrey, 2007, *Little Green Book of Getting Your Way,* FT Press

Gitomer, Jeffrey, 2007, *Little Platinum Book of Cha-Ching!*, FT Press

Gitomer, Jeffrey, 2007, *Little Gold Book of Yes! Attitude*, FT Press

Gladwell, Malcolm, 2005, *Blink*, Penguin

Gladwell, Malcom, 2008, *Outliers,* Penguin

Gladwell, Malcom, 2000, *The Tipping Point*, Abacus

Goldratt, E. M; Cox, J, 1984, *The Goal*, Gower

Grieve, Bradley T., 2008, *Thank You for Being You*, BTG Studios

Hamilton, Roger, 2006, *Your Life Your Legacy*, Achievers

Hancock, Jonathan, 2011, *Brilliant Memory Training*, Pearson

Hardy, Darren, 2010, *The Compound Effect*, Success

Harv Eker. T, 1996, *Speedwealth,* Peak Potentials

Harv Eker. T, 2005, *Secrets of the Millionaire Mind: Mastering the Inner Game of Wealth,* Harper Collins

Heller, Robert, 2001, *Managing for Excellence*, Dorling Kindersley

Hicks, Esher & Jerry, 2006, *The Secret Law of Attraction,* Hay House

Hicks, Esher & Jerry, 2008, *Money and the Law of Attraction*, Hay House

Hill, Napoleon, 1966, *Think and Grow Rich*, Wilshire Books

Hill, Napoleon, 1995, *Positive Action Plan*, Piatkus

Hodgkinson, Liz, 2006, *The Complete Guide to Investing in Property*, Kogan

Jay, Ros, 1995, *How to Build a Great Team, Prentice Hall*

Johnson, K. L, 1993, *Selling with NLP*, Positive

Kaplun, R. S; Norton, D. P, 2004, *Strategy Maps*, HBS Press

Kellaway, Lucy, 2007, *The Answers*, Profile

Kiyosaki, Robert , 2000, *Rich Dad Poor Dad*, Sphere

Kiyosaki, Robert , 2000, *Rich Dad's Guide to Investing*, Timewarner

Koch, Richard, 2004, *Living the 80/20 way*, Nicholas Brealey

Koch, Richard, 1997, *The 80/20 Principle*, Nicholas Brealey

Krause, D. G, 1996, *Sun Tzu: The Art of War for Executives*, Nicholas Brealey

Krogerus, M; Tschappler, R, 2011, *"The Decision Book"*, Pearson

Larson Alan, 2003, *Demystifying Six Sigma*, Amacom

Le Boeuf, Micheal, 1986, *How to Motivate People*, Sidwick & Jackson

Leigh, Andrew , 2008, *The Charisma Effect*, Pearson

Leighton; Kilbey; Bill, 2011, *101 Days to Make a Change: Daily Strategies to Move from Knowing to Being*, Crown House

Livingston, I; Thomson, J, 2007, *Train Your Brain in Seven Days*, Icon

Martin, Curly, 2001, *The Life Coaching Handbook*, Crown House

Matthews, Dan, 2007, *Starting & Running a Business All in One for Dummies*, Matthews

Maxwell, John C., 2003, *Thinking for a Change*, Warner

Mayne, Brian, 2006, *Goal Mapping*, Watkins

McConnell, 2005, *Make Money Be Happy*, Pearson

McCormack, M. H, 1984, What *They Don't Teach You at Harvard Business School*, Collins

McIntosh, Ron, 1993, *The Greatest Secret*, White Stone

McKenna, Paul, 2006, *90 Day Success Journal*, Bantam

Milligan, A; Smith, S, 2006, *See Feel Think Do*, Marshall Cavendish

Mullingan, Eileen, 1999, *Life Coaching Change Your Life in 7 Days*, Piatkus

O'Connell, Fergus, 2008, *How to Get More Done*, Pearson

Oech, R. von , 1983, *A Whack on the side of the Head*, Hachette

Olson, Jeff, 2005, *The Slight Edge*, Success

Owen, Jo, 2010, *How to Tell*, Prentice Hall

Owen, Nick, 2004, *More Magic of Metaphors,* Crown House

Owen, Nick, 2004, *The Magic of Metaphors*, Crown House

Ozaniec, Naomi, 1997, *101 Essential Tips: Everyday Meditation*, Dorling Kindersley

Parkes Cordock, R, 2006, *Millionaire Upgrade*, Capstone

Parkin, J. C, 2007, *Fuck It,* Hay House

Pease, Allan & Barbara , 2004, *The Definitive Book of Body Language*, Orion

Peck, M. Scott, 1990, *The Road Less Travelled*, Arrow

Peeling, Nic, 2005, *Brilliant Manager*, Pearson

Periklis, Mark, 2010, *The Insiders Guide to Buying Property in Difficult Times*, Filament

Richardson, Pam, 2004, *Life Coach*, Hamlyn

Roberts, Graham, 2003*, Law Relating to Financial Services*, IFS

Rowntree, Derek, 1996*, The Manager's Book of Checklists,* Pearson

Searle, Sue, 2012*, Affirmations for Success*, Amazon

Senge, Peter M., 1990, *The Fifth Discipline*, Century Business

Senger, H. von 2004, *The 36 Strategies of Business*, Marshall Cavendish

Silbinger, Steven, 1999, *The 10-Day MBA*, Piatkus

Streibel, Barbara. J, 2003, *The Manager's Guide to Effective Meetings*, Briefcase

Strutely, Richard, 1999, *The Definitive Business Plan*, Prentice Hall

Templar, Richard, 2005, *The Rules of Management*, Pearson

Thaler, R. H; Sunstein, C. R, 2008, *Nudge,* Caravan

Tom, D; Barrons, B. R., 2006, *The Business General: Transform your business using seven secrets of military success,* Vermillion

Tracy, Brian, 2001, *Eat That Frog*, Berret Koehler

Turner, Catherine, 2001, *Personal Lending & Mortgages*, Financial World

Turner, Colin, 1997, *Swimming with Piranha makes you Hungry*, InToto

Turner, Colin, 1994, *Born to Succeed*, Element

Vickers; Bavister; Smith, 2009, *Personal Impact*, Pearson

Virtue, Doreen, 2006, *Angels 101*, Hay House

Virtue, Doreen, 2007, *How to Hear Your Angels,* Hay House

Walsh, Ciaran, 1996, Key Management Ratios, Prentice Hall

Wasmund, S with Newton . R, 2012, *Stop Talking Start Doing,* Capstone Publishing Ltd.

Watkins, Micheal, 2003, *The First 90 Days*, HBS Press

Wattles, Wallace D., 1976, *The Science of Getting Rich*, Destiny

Webb, Phillip & Sandra, 1999, *The Small Business Handbook*, Prentice Hall

Welch, Jack, 2005, *Winning*, Harper Collins

Welch, Suzy, 2009, *10 Minutes 10 Months 10 Years: A Life Transforming Idea*, Simon & Schuster

Whitmore, John, 1992, *Coaching for Performance*, Nicholas Brealey

Whitney, Russ, 1984, *Overcoming*, Whitney Leadership Group

Whitney, Russ, 1995, *Building Wealth*, Fireside

Williams, Nick, 1999, *The Work We Were Born To Do*, Element

Wilson, Derek, 1988, *Rothschild* , Andre Deutch

Wiseman, Richard, 2003, *The Luck Factor*, Arrow

Wood, Frank, 1967, *Business Accounting 1*, Prentice Hall

Yeung, Rob, 2008, *Confidence,* Pearson

Yeung, Rob, 2009, *Personality,* Pearson

Made in the USA
Columbia, SC
20 April 2017